# LEADERSHIP IN A SYNODAL CHURCH

ANNE BENJAMIN & CHARLES BURFORD

Published in Australia by
Garratt Publishing
32 Glenvale Crescent
Mulgrave, VIC 3170
www.garrattpublishing.com.au

Copyright in this work remains the property of the contributing authors.

Copyright © 2021 Anne Benjamin & Charles Burford

All rights reserved. Except as provided by the Australian copyright law, no part of this book may be reproduced in any way without permission in writing from the publisher.

Design by Guy Holt
Edited by Greg Hill
Cover image by iStock
Photographs © iStock on Contents page and pp 2, 5, 10, 18, 23, 28, 31, 38, 51, 53, 56, 64, 72, 79, 82
All other photographs provided by the authors. Anne & Charles would like to thank and acknowledge the permission to use these photos from the following sources: Shuttlestock, Dreamstime, Diocese of Parramatta, Catholic Schools Office, Maitland-Newcastle, Catholic School Parents Australia, St Joseph's Sorrento, National Catholic Commission NCEC.

Printed by Tingleman Printers

All rights reserved.

ISBN 9781925009224

 A catalogue record for this book is available from the National Library of Australia

The authors and publisher gratefully acknowledge the permission granted to reproduce the copyright material in this book.
Every effort has been made to trace copyright holders and to obtain their permission for the use of copyright material.

The publisher apologises for any errors or omissions in the above list and would be grateful if notified of any corrections that should be incorporated in future reprints or editions of this book.

*'Towards an Adult Church' was the mantra of an Archdiocesan Adult Education Centre where I worked thirty years ago. Leadership in a Synodal Church shows us what an adult Church looks like. The authors, modelling what they desire, look through the lens of leadership, and the best of contemporary leadership theory, to explore what the Church could be and should be if true to its mission. An adult Church is one in which members are not mere collaborators but are co-responsible for the life and mission of the Church. To become adult the Church must undergo cultural change so that it more truly aligns with God's mission. Pope Francis calls for such a Church – a synodal Church characterised by mutuality, transparency and accountability. The book does not shy away from the complexities, competing loyalties and diverse expectations that Church leaders must face. By offering theoretical frameworks, processes and activities in support of Church leaders, it offers hope.*

— **Sr Patty Fawkner SGS, Congregational Leader**

*Whether you are beginning your leadership journey or at the forefront of your respective ecclesial ministry, one must acknowledge and appreciate the essence of leadership within the context of a volatile, uncertain, complex and ambiguous world – yet muster the courage to forge on to unravel the great characteristics of synodality within our contemporary Church. The Authors Anne Benjamin and Charles Burford have researched various models of leadership and clearly articulated a path forward to provoke thought and insights, encourage further dialogue, and spend time in reflection and discernment. I highly recommend this book as a resource for leveraging, learning from and growing in leadership – serving our community in the likeness of Christ.*

— **Padmi Pathinather, Chairperson, Diocesan Pastoral Council, Diocese of Parramatta**

*Leadership in a Synodal Church is a timely contribution to a crucial feature of church life in an unfolding era of church renewal, and it is energised by the vision of Pope Francis for a synodal model of church. Pope Francis defines 'synodality' as 'not some of the bishops some of the time but all of the people all of the time'. This book brings together this vision of solidarity with a distillation of learnings about leadership.*
*Dr Anne Benjamin and Dr Charles Burford are highly qualified to write this book [with their] leadership wisdom and considerable experience working in diverse aspects of church life. Although there is a general pessimism about the decline of Christianity in the Western world, including Catholicism, there are encouraging signs now of the Spirit leading the people of God to recover New Testament models of leadership with the insights of contemporary leadership studies. In this book the Activity Exercises provide opportunities to ground the expanse of leadership literature with day-to-day living out of the ideals of leadership exemplified by Jesus. I would hope that all Catholic institutes and agencies utilise the insights of this book to ensure there is a congruency between styles and practices of leadership, and the mission of Jesus for the reign of God.*

— **Dr Kevin Treston OAM**

*In Leadership in A Synodal Church Burford and Benjamin make a forthright, well-researched and deeply scriptural and spiritual contribution to expanding and renewing the sacred role of leadership in the Church. Their call to locate every single aspect of Christian ministry in the mission of the Church, and the person and message of Jesus of Nazareth, provides firm confidence for a Church that constantly strives to be at its best whilst knowing that at times it will fail. This book has the potential to bless and inform those individuals and organisations that take the time to savour its wisdom.*

— **Philip Pogson FAICD - Company Director and Christian school Chair**

*The strength of any organisation depends on the way it is managed, and while the church as an organisation is about beliefs and faith, it still needs good leadership and sound governance. Anne Benjamin and Charles Burford not only expose the shortcomings in church leadership and governance but, more importantly, their book also offers concrete and contemporary solutions. Benjamin and Burford's book is a must-have for anyone involved in the church.*

— **Fr Joseph Lam, Parish Priest of Glenbrook, former Professor of Patristic and Theology at the Lateran University and Australian Catholic University**

*This book is a 'must read' for anyone involved in church governance or leadership. The authors have skilfully brought together contemporary scholarship in theology, leadership and organisational theory to inspire those looking to refocus the church on its core mission consistent with the vision of Pope Francis for a genuinely participative church.*

— **David Hutton OAM, Executive Director Emeritus of Catholic Education, Archdiocese of Brisbane**

*In a Church beset by uncertainty and instability, this book offers the discerning reader many moments of discovery. Relying on time-tested knowledge and theories of leadership – especially in an educational context – the authors present genuinely new ideas and constructs about how to perceive, think about and blend together ministry, culture and leadership in the contemporary Catholic Church, and the result is provocative and engaging. Highly recommended!*

— **Dr Lauretta Baker RSJ, Congregational Leader, Sisters of St. Joseph, Lochinvar**

*From its outset this book promises to be 'an invitation to explore ministry within the contemporary Catholic Church through the lens of leadership' with a key goal of promoting a more synodal Church by building on existing good practice. It delivers what it promises! Importantly, the authors do not take a deficit view of current leadership in Church ministries, which is both refreshing and enlivening. At the same time, they do not shy away from highlighting what have, on occasions, been egregious examples of poor leadership.*
*This is a stimulating book. It's accessibility and coherence quickly drew me in. Each chapter can stand on its own as a source of deeper understanding, reflection and challenge. It beautifully balances intellectual rigour with insights gleaned from the wisdom and experience of practitioners in current and diverse Australian ministries.*
*The book exemplifies the leadership it advocates – courageous and hopeful. It ... recognises and understands the 'grey' in which all leaders must operate, it draws you towards an honest, intimate examination of your own leadership practice. All the while, it is gentle, encouraging and sustaining.*
*My leadership has been enriched through this book. I will be returning to it again and again.*

— **Dr Lee-Anne Perry AM Executive Director, Queensland Catholic Education Commission**

*This publication provides a great way of exploring synodal leadership in the context of the many areas of the church's engagement with society [an engagement] shaped by God's mission as realised in Jesus Christ through the working of the Holy Spirit.*

— **Teresa Brierley, Director Pastoral Ministries, Diocese of Maitland-Newcastle**

*Leadership in a Synodal Church brings the insights of modern leadership theory to the task of building a new synodal church in accordance with Pope Francis' vision. It is a readable and timely companion for many thousands of church leaders across Australia who bear this responsibility.*

— **Paul McClintock, Chair of SVHA (St Vincent's Health Australia)**

*The Burford and Benjamin book* Leadership in a Synodal Church *gives an excellent insight on leadership theory and its practical application in church leadership. It clearly illustrates just what's possible when true accountability, transparency and inclusion are embraced and lived.*

— **Kathleen McCormack, Founding Director CatholicCare Diocese of Wollongong, Member of the Pontifical Commission for the Protection of Minors 2014-2017, Member of the Implementation Advisory Group, March 2018-August 2020**

*This book,* Leadership in a Synodal Church, *offers practical suggestions for diverse expressions of ministry in our Australian Church at a time when this is most needed. It is grounded in a review of contemporary theological understanding and challenge and it provides a comprehensive critique of leadership theory and practice related to ministry. It will be a valuable Australian resource for all in ministry, filling a gap in parish and diocesan ministry and augmenting ministries in education, health and social services in the vital area of understanding ministry.*

— **Phil Billington, Ministry without Borders**

*Critical in the ongoing renewal of the Church is attention to leadership that is culturally aware, relationally focused and characterised by synodality — three potentially elusive elements. This book opens up, with clarity and imagination, things we aspire to but struggle to realise.*

— **Professor Br David Hall fms, Dean, La Salle Academy, Australian Catholic University**

# Contents

Introduction .................................................................................................. 2

Chapter 1
   Leadership for Mission ........................................................................... 5

Chapter 2
   Contemporary Issues of Culture and Leadership in the Church ........ 14

Chapter 3
   Mission and Culture ............................................................................. 23

Chapter 4
   The Culture of a Synodal Church ........................................................ 31

Chapter 5
   Cultural, Transrelational and Synodal Leadership ............................. 39

Chapter 6
   Governance Serving Mission in a Synodal Church ............................ 49

Chapter 7
   People in Leadership ............................................................................ 57

Chapter 8
   Leading Through Moral Discernment ................................................ 64

Chapter 9
   Moral Decision-making ....................................................................... 73

Chapter 10
   Developing Leadership for a Synodal Church .................................... 83

Acknowledgements .................................................................................... 89

List of Activities ......................................................................................... 90

List of Diagrams, Figures & Tables ........................................................... 90

Further Reading ......................................................................................... 91

About the Authors ..................................................................................... 92

# Introduction

A time of crisis can be a time when we see the best of who we are. A crisis can also be a time that reveals people of leadership who call to the best in the rest of us. We have seen this in emergencies when ordinary people come forward to rescue those in peril during a local or even a national crisis. These 'ordinary people' may include those digging for people buried under mudslides or collapsed city buildings, and the lone man who dives into surf to assist a swimmer fighting off a shark attack. In crises uncertainty can provoke our best, but also our less-than-best selves. These can be times when we look for leadership and find it wanting, unable to rise above political interest or put formalities of roles aside; unable to recognise and respond to the confusion of those most affected.

In many ways, our society is experiencing both crisis and uncertainty. This is not just arising from the immediate situation of a pandemic. As commentators have suggested, the pandemic has simply shown up the cracks and fragilities already existing in society, including in a nation as comfortable and stable as Australia. We still have, however, longer-term crises including climate devastation, the uneven distribution of wealth and essential goods and services, uncertainty about democracy, and the volatility of our societies.

At the same time, the Catholic Church is experiencing its own time of crisis and uncertainty. Around the world, even long-serving faithful Church members are asking: what is the Church's future? Will it survive its own mismanagement of the sexual abuse of children in Australia, Ireland, the United States, Germany and elsewhere? Will people return to the pews when the COVID-19 crisis diminishes? These, too, are only the immediate presentations of crisis and uncertainty. The cracks and dissatisfactions within the Church have been there for years. The revelation of the extent of abuse in the Church has opened further a wound that has been festering for a long time. It is very easy for those of us who are faithful committed members of our Church to imagine ourselves as lying under the rubble of a disintegrating apartment block, or swimming in the deep while being circled by sharks, trying to resist the inclination to let go, to sleep, to drown, rather than continue our efforts to be Church. Too pessimistic, some might say. The fact is, this is a critical time for our Church in the midst of a society faced with uncertainty. The two are inseparable. Typically, society would rightly expect religious groups, including the Catholic Church, to reach out and offer leadership and wisdom in these socially uncertain and sometimes chaotic times. Ironically, just when such wise leadership could be helpful, the Church has lost much of its credibility in the eyes of many in society. Consequently, the Church has lost its voice. Some would even argue it has lost its right to have a voice.

All this sounds grim. Fortunately, it is not the full story: in the midst of these realities, the Church — in its various communities and in the lives of the faithful — is alive to its mission. In 2009, when addressing leaders of religious institutes in Australia, Stephen Bevans described the Church in the United States as 'a complex church of many cultures and a rich history'. And while scarred by scandal, it was still 'a church that is incredibly vibrant and alive, especially at the grassroots level'.[1] The description certainly could be applied to the Australian Church of today and, we suspect, to the Church in many other parts of the world.

In such times, more than ever, leadership is needed: leadership that is courageous, insightful, compassionate, resourceful and principled. Through this book, we wish to offer to the Church resources of research and practice in leadership as one contribution to working our way through the complexity of these times. We hope that this book can come to be seen as helping to clear away the rubble with full knowledge that the resources contained within are just small elements in a much larger task of renewal.

In this book we write about leadership in the Church, but it is about leadership in a Church which can be characterised as 'synodal'. When Pope Francis first began using the term 'synodality', it was a term with which many Church members were unfamiliar. Being who he is, Pope Francis did not introduce his emphasis on 'synodality' in a treatise, but instead he shared it bit-by-bit in various talks, papers and reflections over a number of years, building towards a focus on 'synodality' in the Synod of Bishops scheduled for October 2022. Although some commentators note some ambiguity in the Pope's application of the term and how it might be operationalised in our Church, his insistence that synodality is a 'constitutive element of the Church' inspires the key focus of this book.

Synodality is a process which is always spiritual and prayerful as well as collaborative and cooperative. Pope Francis describes it as a process of conversion whereby our Church discerns the reforms necessary for its continuing mission. While synodality will later be discussed in more detail, a useful starting point in understanding its meaning is to view the Church as 'nothing other than the 'journeying together' of God's flock along the paths of history towards the encounter with Christ the Lord'.[2]

The study of leadership over the past fifty years has produced a number of notable models. However typically we use the term 'leadership' to include the meaning of 'an influencing relationship'. In other words, leadership is essentially about people. It is relational and exerts its influence within community in a way which enhances people's humanity. It permeates all aspects of an organisation's life.

For our purposes here, we distinguish between 'leadership' and 'management', or 'administration'. There are many programs offered to executives under the heading of leadership which are more about the business of management and administration than they are about leadership. Competent management and administration are essential in effective organisations. They address important elements such as efficiencies, compliance and reporting, but they are also concerned with how an organisation deploys and treats its people, finance and services. They are tools at the service of mission, vision, values and strategic outcomes: necessary to support the mission but not sufficient to promote it. Our focus in this book will be on leadership that shapes, changes and promotes a cultural synodality in our beloved Church.

A question we asked ourselves in approaching this topic relates to the self-understanding of those in different formal (commissioned) ministerial roles. Do these women and men see themselves as leaders in their Church? Certainly, those in formal leadership positions in the large agencies of Catholic schools, health and welfare are familiar with seeing themselves and being seen as leaders. Can we say the same for those in parish-based or diocesan-based roles, for example Pastoral Parish Council members, Youth ministers? Do they see themselves as leaders in ministry and do their ordained colleagues see them thus?

We will explore the central role of culture in community, how culture is shaped and the role of leaders in shaping and sustaining culture in a desired direction. Culture in an organisation is commonly described as 'the way we do things around here'. It is reflected in practices; in the way people speak, interact, describe themselves and each other; in what is celebrated and how; and in what is rewarded. To ignore culture, to let it take its own course, can result in outcomes totally contrary to an organisation's beliefs, values and rhetoric, as we are painfully aware following the tragic revelations of the recent Australian Royal Commission into Institutional Responses to Child Sexual Abuse (and similar examinations in other countries).

## Laity/laos

'Laity' derives from the word *laos* – meaning the tribe or the people (as in the whole nation). There is a complexity within the term 'laity'. This complexity arises from the two differing uses of *laos*: (i) to distinguish the faithful from those who are ordained and in an approved religious function, and (ii) when referring to the 'People of God'. The Church as the 'People of God' was one of the most powerful theological concepts emerging from Vatican II. As the People of God, all the baptised together form the *laos* – the people – and all share in the three-fold ministry of Christ as Priest, Prophet and King. As Pope John Paul II wrote in 1988, all the faithful, that is the unordained, together with the clergy and women and men consecrated religious, make up the one People of God and the Body of Christ.[3] Vatican II celebrated this in the Constitution on the Church.[4] The purpose of the Constitution on the Church, explained Myriam Wijlens, was to emphasise that 'the Church as such and as a whole has a missionary task and that the hierarchy stands in service to this'[5]. Or as Pope Francis expressed very early in his pontificate, 'All the baptised, whatever their position in the Church or their level of instruction in the faith, are agents of evangelisation.'[6]

However, 'laity' is used most commonly simply to differentiate the non-ordained from the ordained in the Church, without its richer usage as developed in the theology of Vatican II. This perpetuates misunderstanding, or at least limited understanding. Those called to ordained ministry are themselves called from within the *laos* to their service of the Church. *Laos* includes all the People of God: those called to consecrated life and those called to live out their faith in single or married life, as well as those called to ordained ministry. It is time to find another word. Too often, this common use of the term carries associated implications of 'lay' as opposed to 'professional'.

Likewise, it is past time for the Church to find a word to describe those who are usually referred to as 'non-ordained.' 'Non-ordained' is a negative, describing one thing that members of the faithful are not. And just as other negative terms, such as 'non-Australian' and 'non-Catholic', are no longer acceptable terms, neither is 'non-ordained' or 'unordained'. Throughout this book, we will endeavour to avoid both 'laity' and 'non-ordained'.

## A word on our focus

The particular orientations that we bring to the writing of this book are primarily those of education and pastoral life in dioceses and parishes and related organisations. If what we share also resonates in any way with those who lead in other areas of mission, such as health, social services and other ministries, we will be well pleased.

## A note on improved administrative practice

While it is not the focus of this book, we have observed that the Church in some dioceses and parishes would be well-served by improved administrative and management processes. This includes improved communications such as timely responses to correspondences; improved meeting and administration processes; the use of inclusive language in communications; and better planning for leadership succession in significant roles when the end-dates of current appointees are known (for example, the timely re-appointment of bishops, parish priests and Chairs of diocesan bodies). We suspect we are not alone in having firsthand experience of the deleterious impact upon mission and pastoral activity that result from administrative inefficiency.

We invite you through this book to explore the notion of a synodal Church through the lens of leadership. Our goal is to serve the Church's mission by offering a resource that contributes to enhancing leadership in a way which is consistent with a synodal Church and which promotes such synodality. We acknowledge existing good practice in synodal leadership in ministries in the Australian Church; our hope is to build on that by exploring how awareness of leadership theory and good practice can promote a more synodal Church.

## Endnotes

1. Stephan Bevans, SVD, The mission has a Church, the mission has ministers, *Thinking missiologically about ministry and the shortage of priests*, Compass 43, 2009, http://compassreview.org/spring09/2.pd

2. Bishop Mario Grech, quoted in Alessandro Gisotti, A Synod is always a missionary crossroad for the Church. An interview with the Pro-Secretary General of the Synod of Bishops on the value of synodality in Pope Francis' Pontificate and his experience of the Amazonian Synod, *Vatican News*, 2 Nov 2019, https://www.vaticannews.va/en/vatican-city/news/2019-11/grech-synod-crossroads-church-amazon.html

3. Pope John Paull II, Post-synodal Apostolic exhortation, *Christifideles Laici*, on the vocation and mission of the lay faithful in the Church and in the world, (hereafter 'CL') #28, 30 December 1988. http://www.vatican.va/content/john-paul-ii/en/apost_exhortations/documents/hf_jpii_exh_30121988_christifideles-laici.html

4. *LG*, Chapter 2. As mentioned elsewhere, Vatican II stood astride different, and not always consistent, theologies and resolved them by simply placing them side by side. In this case, Chapter 2 on the People of God is followed by Chapter 3 on the Church's hierarchical structure. Likewise, the Congregation for Clergy's 2020 Instruction on the parish seems to speak of co-responsibility and synodality in a rather bureaucratic voice. See Congregation for Clergy, *Instruction, The pastoral conversion of the Parish community in the service of the evangelising mission of the Church*, 20 July 2020, (hereafter' Instruction on parish'). https://press.vatican.va/content/salastampa/en/bollettino/pubblico/2020/07/20/200720a.html

5. Myriam Wijlens, Primacy-Collegiality-Synodality. Refiguring the Church because of *sensus fidei*, reprint from Peter Szabo, ed., *Primacy and Synodality: Deepening Insights, Proceedings of the 23rd Congress of the Society for the Law of the Eastern Churches*, September 3-8, 2017, p. 245.

6. Pope Francis, *Evangelii Gaudium, The Joy of the Gospel*, (EG) November 2013, #120

# Chapter 1
# Leadership for Mission

In any organisation, leaders are called to serve the purpose for which the organisation exists. Likewise, leaders in the Church are called to serve the purpose for which the Church exists.

## The Back Story

In the beginning, before time was measured, the Spirit of God hovered over the waters, over the darkness and formlessness of the earth, breathing into them life and shape, colour and light. Through the ages, this sacred Spirit breathed into the hearts of those who searched for truth; and spoke to nations whose leaders yearned for wisdom and knowledge through prophecy.[1] Then, in time, 'God's ever-present Spirit' took physical form in a Palestinian called Jesus in an out-of-the-way village called Nazareth, and the action of God's Spirit became the mission of Jesus. As Bevans writes, in 'speaking words of wisdom and prophecy, offering God's healing and forgiveness, revealing God's loving but challenging presence in people's lives,' Jesus gives the Spirit of God a 'human face'.[2]

Over the course of a very short public life, Jesus moved amongst the people, teaching and healing: he observed the law as a practising religious Jew. He prayed alone, spent time in communion with his God. He called a small group of women and men to become his friends, to travel with him, to share in his work. He began to teach as a prophet about God and God's Kingdom. When Jesus spoke of God, he spoke about a Father, 'Abba', using a word akin to the familial terms, *Appa, Tatay, Aabbe, Tamai, el Papa, Dad.*[3] The Holy One of Israel was a God with whom Jesus was intimately close. Emboldened in that union in God, Jesus knew 'the liberating power that can challenge all oppressive patriarchal structures and offer new possibilities for a profoundly relational way of life grounded in divine compassionate love'[4].

While some of his listeners in the oppressed situation of 1st century Palestine longed for a political coup, Jesus' mission was a religious one. He brought a religious message that was startling because at its core was the conviction that the all-holy all-powerful God of the Israelites had compassion for the ordinary lives of the simplest people. When Jesus spoke about the Kingdom, he spoke, in José Pagola's words, of his yearning for 'the defeat of evil, the irruption of God's mercy, the elimination of suffering, the acceptance of those previously excluded from community life, the establishment of a society liberated from all affliction'[5]. Denis McBride wrote that Jesus addressed his message to those whose 'open woundedness is a cry to the graciousness of God'. It is these lost, last and least 'who are hugged into importance by an eccentric king who cherishes them above all others. These are the ones who are surprised by love and beneficence in the parables of the Kingdom.'[6]

The religious purists were threatened by Jesus' teaching about a God who lifted burdens from people and who favoured the poor and powerless. After about only three years of his teaching, healing and working with a small team of disciples, he was killed as a criminal. Yet, after three days, people saw him again, risen, alive.

There is an intimacy in shared spiritual experiences. As they discussed amongst themselves their experience and memory of Jesus, the early Christians formed spiritual connections with each other through the deep relationship they held with Jesus, the communion they had formed with him, and with each other. Their encounters with Jesus and his immediate followers highlighted that they were all children of the same loving Father-God of whom Jesus had spoken. Gradually, the community of believers came to the imponderable realisation that, just as the all-holy God had reached out into the world through the Spirit and through Jesus the Word of God, so they were being sent out to continue this mission.[7] This became the communion in the Divine that binds members of the Church and gives the Church its mission.[8]

The experience of Pentecost confirmed their understanding of this mission[9] in recording the early Church's moment of conviction from which there was no going back. We read of their response in the Acts of the Apostles, how they began teaching, first in Israel and then further afield; how the original Twelve apostles and the original band of Jesus' followers grew as the good news spread.[10] Thus, the mission emerged – to continue the work Jesus had begun.

## The mission of the Church: to work towards the Kingdom

The Church was called into existence by the mission entrusted to the early believers. In the words of Stephen Bevans, 'Mission comes first. The church does not have a mission. The mission, rather, has a church. The mission is first that of God's mission – through the Spirit, in Christ. We have been called into the church to share and continue that mission.' This is powerfully expressed in the image of German theologian Emil Brunner whom Bevans quoted as stating 'the church exists by mission as a fire exists by burning'[11].

Vatican Council II (Vatican II) summarised this mission succinctly, even if a little mysteriously: 'For it is the function of the Church, led by the Holy Spirit, who renews and purifies her ceaselessly, to make God the Father and his Incarnate Son present and in a sense visible.'[12] This is both simple and awesome. It implies that the role of each member of the Church is to show to our world – our neighbourhood, fellow workers, our children, our clients and our lovers – something of the divine, the holy, the sacred; something that leads them to 'see' Jesus more clearly. When we pause to consider this mandate, it can be quite confounding.

Another way of describing this mission is to say that the Church came into being because Jesus asked his friends to continue what he had begun: to proclaim the good news he taught in deed and word, 'to establish among all peoples the kingdom of God'[13]. As individual faithful members and as a whole

community (or community of communities), the Church's mission is one of 'evangelisation'. And by 'evangelisation', we simply understand that we have heard what Jesus taught, we cherish the knowledge of a loving God that he showed in his life and we want to share that good news with others. 'Let everyone know,' he urges at the end of Mark's gospel. 'This is really something that will make a difference in people's lives.'[14]

The Kingdom Jesus taught is both in the here-and-now and still-to-be-realised. It is in tension between already-present and not-yet fulfilled until the final coming of God's reign in glory when all will be as it should be in accord with God's will. We see the joy of the Kingdom present all around us. In writing this text, we shared our own experiences of witnessing this joy: the peace in the eyes of the widow, who has been able to forgive those who brutally murdered her husband along with their two small sons, and who returned to continue her missionary work in India; the persistence of those working for more just structures and policies in our country and beyond; the vitality of those who, having suffered enormous injuries, who laugh with gratitude for the gifts they enjoy; in the wisdom of Indigenous peoples in their respect for the earth; in the love of parents for their children in all the unanticipated complications of their lives; and in many ordinary and extraordinary ways and people.

At the same time, we are painfully aware that Jesus' vision of the Kingdom of God is far from being realised.[15] Life and death struggles engross our world: from the groaning of the earth itself in the face of its tenuous future; through the death-bearing maladies of war, hunger, oppression and disease; to the personal struggles of individuals for respect, justice and healing. The daily news gives us images of those struggles between death and life; stories of good wrestling with negative forces while our own personal struggles over life and death are lived out, mostly hidden from public view by the niceties and restraints of social interactions.

Jesus too had to struggle: against crippling and demonising spirits in those who suffered; against temptations to exhibitionism, to power, to short-term wins; against the political force of institutional religion threatened by his teaching of a God of love. Richard Lennan wrote of the Kingdom as 'a gift vulnerable to neither the vicissitudes of history nor the inconsistencies of human faithfulness'. We should take heart, he says, from the death of Jesus, because not even that death could 'rupture God's solidarity with humanity'. Lennan went on to quote Walter Kasper's comment that 'Jesus' death is the form in which the Kingdom of God exists under the conditions of this age, the Kingdom of God in human powerlessness, wealth in poverty, love in desolation, abundance in emptiness, and life in death'.[16]

Along the way, as a People, we falter. Our shortcomings as a Church should not surprise us, because while it exists to serve the Kingdom, the Church is not the Kingdom of God. There is comfort in the assurance that as we try to live out our mission, the Spirit of Jesus is with us, speaking to us in myriad ways – not just through the scriptures, teachers of the Church and the lived faith of the Church, but also through friends, words, events, society and nature – calling us back to the task and giving us heart to keep on going. (Of course, this only makes sense in a worldview that is open to the divine and to the intervention of the Spirit.)

Because of the centrality of Jesus' death and resurrection in our faith, the Church is charged, as part of its mission, to witness to our world a positive stance: the power of God's Spirit against all that is negative and of life over death.[17] We do not deny the reality of our experience of brokenness, but in the midst of that, we are invited to live as followers of one who suffered, died, was buried, yet still triumphed over death.

The People of God are called to be people of hope. The message about God's love revealed in Jesus 'is in harmony with the most secret desires of the human heart',[18] and so, the normal healthy human instinct is to reach for what God's Kingdom brings. We can do so with confidence believing that the God that Jesus spoke about does not give up on us women and men, even when we are at our lowest.

## Contemporary Mission of the Church

Bevans summarised succinctly that the Church does not exist for its own sake, to expand or to perpetuate itself. 'The church exists not as an answer, as it were, but as a response – a response to God's call to continue God's loving, redeeming, healing, reconciling, liberating, forgiving, and challenging mission.'[19]

The Church lives out its mission in different ways according to particular times and contexts.[20] We can see in the life of the early followers of Jesus in Acts 2:42-47 how the apostolic Church, fresh in the memory of Jesus and his teaching, was characterised by fellowship and community (*koinonia*), proclamation about Jesus (*kerygma*), remembering him in prayer and breaking bread (liturgia), service to those in need (*diaconia*), teaching (*didache*) and witnessing (*martyria*). Even then, in those first years, the first disciples needed to grow and change in their understanding as we see in Acts 6:1-7, when the Greek members of the community felt their widows were disadvantaged in the distribution of food. The early community adapted its structure and created new ministries, as Frank Brennan has remarked, so as 'to give everyone a place at the table, including the marginalised Hellenists who had been left out by the dominating Hebrews'[21].

The pertinent characteristics of that mission for our time can be found in documents emerging from Vatican II and in subsequent statements. These official statements emphasise a Church that is:

- a community of witnesses, drawn together by the reality of Jesus, inspired by the Word, nourished and celebrated in Eucharist,
- oriented especially towards the poor, the marginalised and those on the edge,

- embracing and ecumenical, engaged with our world, society, including other faith traditions,
- humble and simple in style, mindful that the mission served is not our own but that of Jesus himself,
- enroute like pilgrims, both holy and sinful, always open, under the guidance of the Spirit, to the necessity of conversion, and
- ecologically integrated, embracing stewardship of creation and the common good – an emphasis given by Pope Francis in *Laudato si'*.[22]

The mission of the Church to witness to God's love is always oriented towards the future, while still always engaged with history, seeking to respond to God's Spirit who calls the Church to the service of God's kingdom here and now. While the Church is oriented towards end-times, we also live in 'end-times': our 'now' is the end-time of all that has gone before. Our current world, too, is a place of ambiguity arising from the end-times (*eschata*) of many certainties. Theologian Vitor Westhelle describes the Church as 'the space of grace', a 'conduit of the Spirit'. His image of the community of believers as a space of grace in the pointy end of life is a sustaining one. Because of the Spirit's presence, 'the place of risk, of condemnation, is also the place of healing and salvation'. His view of Church as a community of those who are on the edge, 'barely hanging on to life' might challenge some of our self-understandings as an institutional Church. Through their faith in the presence of Jesus in his Spirit, the community is sustained. A unique identifier for us as Church, even in the midst of the unutterable turmoil, is that the community is 'able to name and be named by their relationship to God and to one another'.[23] This suggests that one responsibility of a leader in such a community is to facilitate such naming and such relationships.

## Mission and leadership in the Church

The origin of the Church's mission in Jesus Christ has implications for leaders within the Church and for the culture of the agencies and organisations they lead. Francis

Moloney, speaking of ordained priesthood, reminds us that 'all conversation about leadership in the Christian tradition must begin and end with the figure of Jesus of Nazareth'.[24] It seems that this applies to all leadership, not only for the ordained but for all leaders in ministries exercised on behalf of the Church. Given their role and influence, leaders in the Church's ministerial outreach – be they pastoral, administrative, health, social services or educational – carry responsibilities in building and promoting organisational cultures that are consistent with – and faithful to – our mission and founder.

Since those involved in ministries on behalf of the Church are called to take part in a mission which is none other than to continue the mission of Jesus, we need to keep returning to discover and re-discover the person of Jesus in the scriptures and the living traditions of our faith. He is the one in whose name our Church exists. He is the one who inspired the founders of religious institutes to establish their ministries. It is his mission that we, as Church, are called to serve, working towards the realisation of God's reign, always in process, always striving towards things as they should be in his Kingdom.

## Jesus and leadership

There are considerable limitations and risks in attempting to look to Jesus to find what we would call 'models of leadership' appropriate for those in ministry. In the first place, our knowledge of particular specifics about the historical Jesus is severely limited. Secondly, the contexts of 1st Century CE and the Church of the 21st Century CE are incompatible. Finally, such search for a ready-made model in the Christian scriptures runs the risk, at least, of a naïve fundamentalism. Having said that, there are some things we know about Jesus and the kind of public ministry he exercised. The gospel of Matthew recounts his teaching that, unlike powerful rulers who lord it over others, his followers are called to a different kind of leadership, that of service, 'just as the Son of Man did not come to be served, but to serve, and to give his life as a ransom for many' (Matthew 20:25-28).

In her study of the leadership of three women doctors of the Church, Christine Cameron cites a number of references to Jesus as 'servant leader'.[25] And, of course, John's Gospel (13:1-17) makes a very powerful statement about this with the account of the washing of the disciples' feet.[26] The recognition that the focus of each evangelist might affect the leadership style described in the different gospels indicates the risks of this approach. It is wiser to remain at a more generalised understanding of the Jesus of the gospels than too literal an analysis.

Consideration of leadership styles which are appropriate for the community of those who follow Jesus are not new. Thomas Shufflebotham SJ, for example, emphasises that the demands of Christian leadership are high. We will come closer to meeting them, he concludes, if 'we are people preoccupied with the compassion of Christ, speaking with the honesty of Christ, in a spirit of faith enlivened by our contemplation of

Christ steadfastly walking towards Jerusalem', graced by the Spirit.[27] In moving towards Jerusalem, we must remember, Jesus was moving towards his suffering and death. Simply said – if not so simply achieved – leadership within and of the Church must *de facto* be grounded in St Paul's experience of missionary discipleship and leadership, recognising that the cross is part of the package. 'I have been crucified with Christ; it is no longer I who live, but Christ who lives in me; and the life which I now live in the flesh I live by faith in the Son of God, who loved me and gave Himself for me.' (Gal 2:21). Paul's conversion and spirituality, grounded in his experience of the Pascal mystery, finds passionate expression in his discipleship and missionary leadership. The Acts of the Apostles makes great adventure reading for those seeking to lead in a Church ministry and sobering insights for those who wish to lead comfortably.

Adelaide priest, the late Denis Edwards, in his exploration of leadership in the local Church in the light of the New Testament, argued that while leadership can be understood as the influence one exerts within a community, New Testament leadership is always 'relational'. For Edwards, New Testament leadership can be characterised as being:

- servant leadership rather than dominating leadership
- non-violent rather than coercive
- leadership from below rather than from above
- participatory rather than unilateral
- empowering rather than overpowering, and
- based on hope in the resurrection of the crucified rather than in one's own achievements.[28]

Since Vatican II (if not before) there have been references to notions of Church leadership that are collaborative. Pope Benedict XVI posited a notion that went beyond collaboration to 'co-responsibility'.[29] Chris Branson and his colleagues examined the Jesus of the gospels as an exemplar of a 'transrelational model' of leadership.[30] Because the model of transrelational leadership is consistent with both Pope Benedict's 'co-responsibility' and Edwards' claim that New Testament leadership is always relational, we will consider this in more detail in Chapters 5 and 8.

These are just some examples of attempts to focus on leadership within a Gospel perspective.[31]

## Mission finds expression in ministries

It is the mission of the Church – the mission of Jesus – that calls out different ministries. Ministries exist to serve that mission. For our purposes here, Thomas O'Meara's description of Christian ministry as 'the public activity of a baptised follower of Jesus Christ flowing from the Spirit's charism and an individual personality on behalf of the Christian community to witness, to serve and realise the Kingdom of God'[32] provides a useful base.

This definition makes it very clear that there are things that are ministry and things which are not. Ministry is a public ecclesial activity; it is inspired by the Spirit working through an individual; it is exercised on behalf of the ecclesial community and therefore carries implicit and explicit authorisation from the community; its purpose is the realisation of the Kingdom. This understanding also makes clear that there is a measure of formality in the call to ministry, either through ordination, consecrated life or commissioning to roles such as pastoral associate, school principal, pastoral council member, agency head.

It is easy for us to see how the 'Kingdom' inspires the Church's agencies of social services, education, healing, community building and working for justice. Theologian Leonardo Boff described the Kingdom preached by Jesus as lying at the heart of all the Church's ministerial outreach. He described Jesus' mission in terms of a 'fundamental project of liberation and freedom'. The Kingdom, as described by Boff, is about 'the liberation of the poor, comfort for those who cry, justice, peace, forgiveness, and love'. And he further describes the kind of leadership that pertains to that Kingdom in stating Jesus 'did not proclaim an established order; he did not call others to be rulers but to be submissive, humble and loyal'. The liberation he brought called for those in power to see themselves as servants and siblings, 'free from the appetite for greater power ... He does not introduce or bless privileges that give rise to classes and divisions between persons ... (His) is the power of love.[33]

The extent of ministerial outreach within the Australian Catholic Church is comprehensive. Catholic schooling across the country engages 96,000 staff to work with 765,000 students in diocesan systemic schools, schools sponsored by religious institutes and schools conducted by Ministerial Public Juridic Persons.[34] Health and welfare figures are approximately the same.[35] Research in 2018 indicated around 220,000 staff are employed across the Church in Australia. (The researchers did not include priests and religious sisters and brothers.)[36] Ordained ministries include diocesan and religious institute priests, both local and from overseas, permanent deacons, and deacons preparing for ordination.

The Church has traditionally exercised its mission through entities known in Canon Law as Public Juridic Persons (PJPs) which authorises specific Church ministries to operate in the name of the Catholic Church. Traditional PJPs include dioceses, parishes and religious institutes (congregations or orders). Within Australia, there are 33 Dioceses including the non-geographic areas of the Chaldean, Maronite, Melkite and Ukrainian Rites, the Military Ordinariate and the Personal Ordinariate of Our Lady of the Southern Cross. Catholic Religious Australia (CRA) reports it has a membership of more than 150 congregations of sisters, brothers and priests who live and work across Australia, comprising over 5,000 women and men who are members of religious institutes.[37]

While leadership of a diocese, parish or religious institute rests respectively with the Bishop, Parish Priest or Leader of the Religious Institute, there are many other leadership roles within dioceses, parishes and religious institutes that all serve the mission of the Church. This includes the ordained ministries of priest and deacon as well as the commissioned ecclesial ministries associated with those engaged in pastoral work, and leaders in education, health and welfare as an activity of a diocese or religious institute. Many Catholic women and men are involved in formal roles as Pastoral Associates; in pastoral planning; liturgy; youth, family and Christian life; social justice, and the administration of dioceses. Those in other associations of faithful, such as the St Vincent de Paul Society, also serve the Church's mission.

As well as having PJPs authorising specific Church ministries to operate in the name of the Catholic Church, during the past three decades another kind of canonical entity, known as 'Ministerial PJPs,' has emerged in the Australian Church (and elsewhere). Ministerial PJPs are legal entities established by religious institutes and approved by Rome for the purpose of carrying forward the mission and charism of their founders through their particular ministry. For example, a number of Ministerial PJPs exercise a ministry of education (such as Good Samaritan Education or Kildare Ministries) while others exercise a ministry of health and/or social services (such as Catholic Healthcare or MercyCare).[38] The Ministerial PJPs have established clear processes for governance by 'colleges' of stewards or trustees, almost all of whom are neither ordained nor members of a religious institute. While the role of Ministerial PJPs is generally not well known at local parish level, they are already very significant in Australian Church leadership and likely to become more so. Their outreach as part of the Church's mission involves many thousands of people, with agencies governed by formally established Boards. There are many leadership roles within these ministries.

Ministry emerges from the life of the Church and its mission and 'is at the service of the Church's engagement with the world'.[39] Forms of ministry change as the Church's mission 'takes on new responsibilities in an ever-changing world'[40] The Church's ministry has already changed significantly, with the shift towards Ministerial PJPs, with the inclusion of greater diversity in those commissioned to ministerial roles and, not least, with the increased involvement of women. It will continue to change – it should continue to change – and, as the Boston Seminar noted, 'there can be no future for the Church which women have not had a pivotal hand in shaping'[41].

We are long past the time in history when leadership in ministry was formally recognised as the exclusive preserve of the ordained and consecrated religious who had taken religious vows. Leadership in ministry belongs to, and is exercised by, members of the *laos*, ordained, consecrated or not. For the purposes of this book, we include as leaders all those engaged in formal roles in the pastoral, administrative, health, education and social service ministries of the Church. The authors recognise the distinctive nature and role of ordained ministry.

## Leadership for mission: leadership from the heart

Leadership in the Church's mission activity is rightly centred on, and draws its inspiration from, the person of Jesus Christ. Perhaps this is what retired parish priest John Crothers meant when he wrote that clerical leadership is only effective when it is internalised and 'becomes a leadership of the heart, and not just a leadership of the head'[42]. We would maintain that such leadership of the heart applies to all leaders in ministry.

For many leaders in the Church, discipleship is the moral core of their personal mission. The logic of signing up for leadership in a ministry is that it flows from one first choosing to be a follower of Jesus, and then choosing to become a disciple. At the same time, we acknowledge that, while this may be the case for many in positions of leadership in the Church's ministries, others might be more comfortable describing themselves in terms of fidelity to the charism and values of a religious institute, which in turn, of course, has its origins in a response to the gospel.

First and foremost, Christian discipleship is relational. 'Being a disciple' presumes that one has perceived an invitation and has responded 'Yes'. For the first disciples, this was immediate and personal: the teacher Jesus sought them out, called them by name and asked them to join him in his mission. As we see, for example, in Matthew 4:18-22 and related accounts, Jesus reached out and befriended those who would follow him. While the response of each disciple to the person of Jesus Christ is intensely personal, in living out that commitment we follow him together as a group, a fellowship, a band of companions strengthening each other in faith, 'never completely ourselves unless we belong to a people'[43].

Seeing oneself as a disciple of Jesus does not mean that answers about leadership or other issues that arise in a leader's life are apparent or easy to find. As friends and followers of Jesus, there are many situations in our everyday lives and relationships that can confront us with confusion or options. This results in tensions which can be at the personal, interpersonal, institutional or cultural level. Let us take as an example from everyday life, something as unremarkable as the choice of high school for a daughter. The tensions parents might need to balance in making their decision could include: their own different educational backgrounds; their different preferences for single-sex as opposed to co-ed schooling especially if they come from different cultural or ethnic backgrounds; a preference for a religious school as opposed to the career advantages of a selective school; cost and the related pressure on the family; as well as the daughter's personality, particular educational requirements and preferences. In working towards a decision, the parents (with their daughter we suggest) would need to work through a discernment process, which is essentially a moral exercise in which they identify these tensions, seek out the facts and then focus on the values involved and which ones they would adopt. There's no easy answer to be found in the gospels about this everyday decision.

Leadership decisions, likewise, are often complex with no apparent right answer. As in the example above, the decision-making path includes identifying the tensions involved, getting the facts, and identifying the values that might be in tension. The final decision might be the one which is least compromised, since moral decisions often need to be made between two less desirable options, rather than simply between one that is good and one that is bad. In trying to live a life faithful to the Jesus of the gospels, one always has to search out the path to follow. Such searching (or discernment) is always in essence deeply spiritual. It demands, in various ways, depending on each situation, an openness to conversion from our own point of view to a perspective that reflects the surprising wisdom of the gospels. This means leadership for mission can very much be a spiritual exercise. And this exercise can be shaped by an awareness that we, as leaders, are stewards, and the decisions we make can impact creation and immediate and wider communities both now and into the future.

## Leadership and moral discernment

In the quiet of one's room at dawn, a leader's purpose might appear clear and evident: a purpose drawn from the mandate of a disciple – or through charism – to promote through word and action the Kingdom Jesus taught, and a life living out the values, ethical beliefs and commitments aligned with that purpose through a ministry of service. This purpose carries a moral character because of its foundation in values and ethical principles. Five minutes into the working day, the simple clarity of that moral purpose can be lost in a fog of multiple imperatives, competing perspectives and yesterday's still-pending agenda.

In many instances, leaders instinctively handle the kind of discernment that is required almost instantaneously; in other instances, the process of discernment requires more focused time and attention. The tension might present as a difficult or under-performing staff member, a belligerent or litigious client, the demands of popular opinion, external legislators, or jurisdictional authorities that are in conflict with the gospel.

Or it might not be clear which path is closer to the gospel. It is indeed salutary to ask and reflect: 'What would Jesus do?' However, the 21st century context, biotechnology, government legislation, medical research possibilities, competitive funding, the sheer pressure of multiple learning needs in one classroom, the scale of some ministries, to name just a few elements, are far removed from the context of 1st century Palestine.

Constant reflection, critique and dialogue are the essence of a leader's discernment. Every budget reflects an expression of values by the organisation. Every leader's diary reflects their judgement of what is of value in their leadership. Evidence of our discipleship is found in how we allocate our time, money and other resources. Leadership presumes a high level of self-awareness, personal honesty and a willingness to reflect. The self-awareness, integrity and reflectiveness that enable a leader to consider some of the questions proposed in resolving tensions arise from, and are fed by, a leader's spirituality. Spirituality is intensely personal, and readers will have their own spirituality underpinning their leadership.

It is salutary to keep in mind that exercising leadership for mission occurs in an increasingly incredulous world.[44] Leadership in promoting the mission of Jesus is counter-cultural and challenging. It is a small voice in a noisy world, but a voice which nonetheless is searching for the connectedness of community and the meaning which faith brings. Being faithful witnesses to God's love can come at a cost, just as it cost the prophets in the Hebrew scriptures who were often ridiculed and isolated.

## Leadership as witness

Within a Christian worldview, leadership is essentially about service towards others and with others. It arises from the call through Baptism and vocation, the commitment to discipleship and the promotion of Jesus' mission. At the same time, being a leader within this faith perspective requires an ongoing commitment to search for more authentic and whole-hearted discipleship. In this way, an individual's exercise of leadership can itself witness to their own journey towards fuller and more authentic discipleship.

Hernán Paredes and Tomas Bradley were young Jesuits at the time that the man who was to become Pope Francis was rector of the Jesuit seminary of Colegio Maximo in Argentina in the mid-1980s. Paredes recalls the rector feeding the pigs. Bradley recalls 'Jorge' as being the man who did the household laundry for a household of more than a hundred. Tomás recalled that 'already at 5:30 in the morning, he (Bergoglio) would be placing clothes into those two industrial washing machines we had.' Is that such a big deal, asks Lowney in recounting this. Perhaps, he suggests, the rector would have been better off spending his time professionally forming future priests and leaders. Lowney concludes: 'That's just it: he was forming leaders and priests ... Hernán Paredes and Tomás Bradley must have seen Bergoglio do and say thousands of things – why do pig-feeding and laundry washing stand out as indelible memories?'[45]

# Activity 1.1: Who is Jesus?

How do you describe Jesus?

*For me, today, this is how I express my understanding of Jesus Christ, a 1st century CE Palestinian observant Jew from an out-of-the-way village called Nazareth in the north of his country, who emerged as a religious prophet and a healer. It is an understanding that has changed over the decades; it will change again, if only in its emphases.*

Jesus taught –
a kingdom that is here and is to come
especially for the hurt, the small, the excluded
a kingdom that embraces all, the 'other'
above all, a kingdom which expresses the reign of God.

And the God he spoke of –
steadfast as Uluru,
loving, strong and determined as a mother,
protective as a mother hen,
who rejoices in the just,
gives joy
moves people to bang tambourines,
break out in song
and even to dance,
is marvellous and beyond our imaginings,
faithful, compassionate, merciful
holy.

Jesus felt the pain of others,
felt it in the pit of his stomach.
He healed,
he gave life where there was death,
he gave hope.

Jesus ate and drank with the B-listers,
the Z-listers and non-listers,
relaxed,
enjoyed his world,
was in this world.
Jesus called some to be his disciples
he challenged his followers
challenged authorities,
was not naïve about the price
and saw the writing on the wall.

Jesus prayed
reflected
went away alone to be with God
sought out his mission.

Jesus respected and observed the law,
he put people before the law,
he challenged law and teachings polluted
by time and custom
he recognised the need for reform.

Jesus was killed as a criminal,
a terrorist of sorts,
from many perspectives, he was a failure
he defied death and yet
lives on in his followers
Death did not kill him
death did not destroy his mission
to bring the kingdom of his God to realisation.

(Anne Benjamin)

## Activity 1.2: What is tenderness?

This is the question Pope Francis asked his TED Talk audience before answering in this way:

It is the love that comes close and becomes real. It is a movement that starts from our heart and reaches the eyes, the ears and the hands. Tenderness means to use our eyes to see the other, our ears to hear the other, to listen to the children, the poor, those who are afraid of the future. To listen also to the silent cry of our common home, of our sick and polluted earth. Tenderness means to use our hands and our heart to comfort the other, to take care of those in need ... This is tenderness: being on the same level as the other ... [Jesus] lived his entire human existence practising the real, concrete language of love. (Pope Francis, TED Talk, 26th April 2017)

- When is it easy in your ministry to exercise this?
- When is it difficult?
- Have you seen others demonstrate these characteristics?
  — Who?
  — When?

## Endnotes

1. Cf. Genesis 1.
2. Bevans.
3. 'Father' in Tamil, Filipino, Somali, Tongan, Spanish.
4. Denis Edwards, *Jesus the wisdom of God*, St Pauls, Homebush, 1995, pp. 48-49.
5. José Antonio Pagola, Jesus, *An historical approximation*, Convivium Press, p. 175.
6. Denis McBride, *Jesus and the gospels*, Redemptorist Publications, Hampshire, 2002, p. 110
7. Vatican Council II, *Ad Gentes*, (hereafter AG), Decree on the Missionary Activity of the Church, #2, in Vatican Council II: *The Conciliar Documents*, A. Flannery, Geoffrey Chapman (eds), London, 1966.
8. Cf. CL #32.
9. Acts 2.
10. Cf. Acts 2:46-47; 13:1-4. Pope John Paul II, Redemptoris mission, 'On the permanent validity of the Church's missionary mandate', #27, (hereafter RM), 7 December 1990, https://w2.vatican.va/content/john-paul-ii/en/encyclicals/documents/hf_jp-ii_enc_07121990_redemptoris-missio.html
11. Bevans.
12. Vatican Council II, *Gaudium et Spes*, (hereafter GS), Pastoral Constitution on the Church in the Modern World, #21, in A Flannery, p. 219.
13. Vatican II Council *Lumen Gentium* (hereafter LG), *The Dogmatic Constitution on the Church*, #5, in A Flannery.
14. Cf. Mark 15:15: CL, #33.
15. RM #1,
16. Richard Lennan, The Church as Mission. Locating vocation in its ecclesial context, (hereafter Lennan, Mission) in *The Disciples' Call: Theologies of Vocation from Scripture to the Present Day*, Christopher Jamison & T & T Clark, London, 2013, e-book, p. 47.
17. LG, #38.
18. GS, #21.
19. Bevans.
20. LG, #1.
21. Frank Brennan, Becoming a Church for mission 2030, closing keynote address at the Catholic Mission Conference, Sydney, 17 May 2017, https://www.eurekastreet.com.au/article/becoming-a-church-for-mission-2030#
22. Pope Francis, *Laudato si* (hereafter LS), On Care for our Common Home, Encyclical Letter, 24 May 2015.
23. Vitor Westhelle, quoted in Lennan, Mission, p. 49.
24. Francis J. Moloney SDB, in *Broken for you. Jesus Christ, the Catholic Priesthood and the Word of God*, Coventry Press, Bayswater, 2018, p..6.
25. Christine Cameron, *Leadership as a Call to Service*, (hereafter Call to Service), Conor Court Publishing, Ballan, 2012, pp.12-13, 250-251.
26. We wouldn't presume to go as far as Blanchard and Hodges, quoted in *Call to Service*, when they write, 'That's what Jesus had in mind when he washed the feet of the disciples.' We don't know this.
27. Thomas Shufflebotham, sj, 'A Reflection on Jesus' Leadership', *Thinking Faith*, 4 July 2012.
28. Denis Edwards, *Called to be Church in Australia*, St Paul's Publications, Homebush, 1987.
29. Pope Benedict XVI, Opening of the Pastoral Convention of the Diocese of Rome on the theme of Church membership and pastoral co-responsibility, 26 May 2009.
30. Chris Branson et al 2019, pp. 223-224 citing Haslam, Reicher and Platow.
31. See also Chris Lowney, *Heroic Leadership*, Loyola Press, Chicago, 2003, Chapter 4, where he explores a model for Christian leadership drawing on the Church of the 1st Century.
32. T. O'Meara, *Theology of Ministry*, Paulist Press, New York, 1983, p. 142.
33. Leonardo Boff, The Power of the Institutional Church – Can it be converted? (1981), extract in Mannion, G, et al (eds), *Readings in Church authority: gifts and challenges for contemporary Catholicism*, Ashgate Publishing, Aldershot, 2003, p. 536.
34. National Catholic Education Commission, *Facts about Catholic Education*, https://www.ncec.catholic.edu.au/resources/the-facts-about-catholic-education, accessed 1 Dec 2019.
35. Catholic Health Australia website, https://www.cha.org.au/about, accessed 1 Dec 2019.
36. Robert Dixon, George Keryk et al, *Our Work Matters*, Australian Catholic Council for Employment Relations. ACCER 2017, https://www.accer.asn.au/ There are additional resources on this site.
37. Cf Website, Catholic Religious Australia, https://www.catholicreligious.org.au/
38. An introduction to Ministerial PJPs can be found on the website of the Association of Ministerial PJPs, https://ampjp.org.au/
39. Richard Lennan, Richard Gaillardetz et al, To serve the people of God: renewing the conversation on priesthood and ministry, Boston College Seminar on Priesthood and the Contemporary Church (hereafter Boston Seminar), *Origins*, 48:31, 2018, p. 487.
40. Boston Seminar, p. 487.
41. Elizabeth Johnson, quoted in Boston Seminar, p. 491.
42. John Crothers, *The Clergy Club*, Garratt Publishing, Melbourne, 2018, p. 17.
43. Cf Pope Francis, *Letter to the People of God*, Vatican, 18 August 2018, #2.
44. United States Catholic Conference, Co-Workers in the Vineyard of the Lord. A Resource for guiding the development of lay ecclesial ministry, USCC, 2005, p. 26.
45. Chris Lowney, *Pope Francis: Why He Leads the Way He Leads*, Loyola Press, Chicago, 2013, pp. 60-61. Lowney is a former Jesuit seminarian, Former Managing Director of J. P. Morgan and Chair of the USA Catholic Health Initiatives Board.

## Chapter 2

# Contemporary Issues of Culture and Leadership in the Church

### A pilgrim Church always in need of reform

From the time of the early Christian communities, the Church, like any dynamic organisation, has experienced constant challenges and the need for renewal. When Pope John XXIII convoked Vatican II in 1959[1], it was for just such a process of renewal. Renewal envisaged by Vatican II was to come from *ressourcement* – a rediscovery of the authoritative sources of Christian faith – and *aggiornamento* – a process of renewal, a freshening up of the Church by opening the windows and letting the Spirit blow through.[2] For those who were young adults immersed in the life of the Church at the time, Vatican II offered promises: a Church grounded in scripture and a tradition of lived (vital) faith, expressed in a liturgy that spoke a familiar language; a Church open to the world, its joys and hopes, its griefs and anxieties – all our human endeavour – with a special place for those who are poor or in any way distressed.[3] It was exciting and inspiring.

Changes followed: Catholic engagement with the scriptures, liturgical reforms, a variety of roles for lay people and greater engagement with other Christian traditions and other religions. The hierarchical formality of the Church, however, did not change, and for many who were caught up in the spirit of Vatican II, the possibilities the Council opened up were not realised. The disappointment following Vatican II – realistic or otherwise – lives on.

The notion of the Church as the 'People of God' was given pre-eminence as Chapter 2 in Vatican II's *Dogmatic Constitution on the Church*: all the people of God, each one of the baptised, share in the priesthood, leadership and prophetic roles of Jesus himself.[4] This holy people, the Constitution continued, is pre-eminently a pilgrim people, nomads and campers, transients on the way towards the coming of God's time of justice, holiness and mercy.⁵ Pope John XXIII might have surprised many with his announcement of a Council within three months of being elected Pontiff. However, no-one in the Church should have been surprised by the call for reform. As Richard Lennan notes, the Church 'can never graduate from its pilgrim status'. We are always on the way towards the Kingdom's eschatological fulfilment. Further, as Church we are in constant need of conversion to overcome our tendency to become a 'counter testimony', to being the sacrament of Jesus and God we are called to be; 'thirdly, the Church is God's work and human initiative alone cannot determine it.' In the Creed we reiterate our belief in the 'holy' Church, which can seem something of a half-statement because we are very much also a 'broken' Church. So, it is heartening to read Lennan's reminder that this is a declaration of faith in God's love for the Church, rather than a declaration of belief in the Church's perfection. 'Our ultimate trust ... is in God, not the Church.'⁶

Move forward to 2020. It is axiomatic that the Church in the 21st century is facing challenges. Not just in Australia, but globally. There is a sense of urgency for reform, renewal and change coming from within the Church, not only from the Pope but also from the grassroots. Much of this revolves around culture. In the secular world of the public domain, likewise, there is a clamour for change in the Church, with attitudes ranging from critical respect, through to a perception the Church has lost all credibility or is totally irrelevant.

Leadership is always an issue for any organisation and is critical at times of challenge and change. If the culture of the Church is to change, a focus on leadership in the Church at this time is an imperative, not an option.

## Sexual abuse in the Church and its implications for leadership

The horror revealed through the Australian Government's Royal Commission⁷ about the extent of sexual abuse of children by members of the Church, especially by its clergy and religious, and the institutional response to that abuse, have shocked us with the failure of Church leadership to deal appropriately with examples of abuse at that time.

In the interests of transparency, the figures are repeated here. The Royal Commission's final report documents that of the 4,029 survivors of child sexual abuse in religious institutions who spoke to the Commission, the largest proportion spoke about child sexual abuse in Catholic institutions – no fewer than 2,489 survivors. Child sexual abuse reported in private sessions occurred in 964 different Catholic institutions. It is salutary for all in the Church to keep these figures in mind. The Royal Commission further concluded that:

> [in] its responses to child sexual abuse, the leadership of the Catholic Church has failed the people of the Catholic Church in Australia, in particular its children ... There were catastrophic failures of leadership of Catholic Church authorities over many decades, particularly before the 1990s.⁸

We have become painfully aware that the failures documented by the Royal Commission have caused enduring suffering for children, their families and the wider communities. People have died, or become profoundly damaged, because of these failures in leadership. And the corollary is that in many instances, 'that harm could have been avoided had Catholic Church authorities acted in the interests of children rather than in their own interests'.⁹

The Catholic Church owes an enormous debt of gratitude to the survivors who made representations to the Royal Commission, to the persistent diligence of the Commissioners and their team, and to then Prime Minister Julia Gillard and the Australian Government, for highlighting in an unavoidable way what the Church had been unable to do for itself. Among the contributing factors to the Report's findings, the Commissioners' findings regarding the operations of the Catholic Church include:

- a culture of clericalism,

- hierarchical and non-transparent organisational governance structures that exclude the contribution of lay women and men,

- failures of leadership in the Church, including non-observance of existing provisions in Towards Healing protocols, appointment processes for bishops, need for leadership training for ordained and religious, and

- poor oversight, lack of accountability processes and absent commitment to ongoing learning by ordained.¹⁰

These factors are all elements of organisational culture and of organisational leadership.

On 20th August 2018, Pope Francis wrote a letter to the People of God. Responding to the dereliction of care for those abused by Church members and leaders around the world, he called each of us and the Church as a whole to conversion. 'No effort to beg pardon and to seek to repair the harm done,' he lamented, will ever be enough. And for the future, 'no effort must be spared to create a culture able to prevent such situations from happening, but also to prevent the possibility of their being covered up and perpetuated'.¹¹ And as leader of the Church, he acknowledged with shame and repentance that 'we were not where we should have been, that we did not act in a timely manner, realising the magnitude and the gravity of the damage done to so many lives'.¹²

Responding to Pope Francis' exhortations on the contemporary Church, Bishop Long has spoken of the need in Australia for a 'bold and strong leadership' to move the People of God towards 'a new culture of humility, accountability and service'.[13] In his response to the Pope, he has called to the local Church for conversion, to change from a clerical culture, to reclaim the priesthood of the faithful and to become a Church oriented to mutuality and partnerships.

In response to the clamouring call to conversion coming to the Church from the secular sphere of the Royal Commission's recommendations, in 2018 the Australian Catholic Bishops Conference (ACBC) and Catholic Religious Australia (CRA) established an Implementation Advisory Group (IAG) to oversee the work of a governance review of the Church. The IAG established a Governance Review Project Team who began their work of review in March 2019, handing down their preliminary report in May 2020 for the consideration of the ACBC and CRA. The final report was published in August 2020.[14] The key topics for the reviewers revolved around leadership and culture, and particularly:

- the interdependence of culture and fidelity to Jesus Christ
- systems, structures and processes of accountability with respect to cultural change
- cultural and governance practices that promote 'proper relational and welcoming institutional systems and processes', and
- how the 'imperatives of co-responsibility, collaboration and genuine consultation' might be realised in a synodal Church.[15]

The Governance review report was incorporated into preparations for the Plenary Council of the Catholic Church in Australia by being made available to those preparing its working papers and planning its agenda.[16] As President of the Australian Catholic Bishops' Conference (ACBC), Archbishop Mark Coleridge indicated that the Plenary Council would determine the Church's response to the report; and added that, 'given that the Council is the work of the Holy Spirit, it is the Holy Spirit who will have the final say'. This did not preclude individual bishops from taking their own decisions and actions before the Plenary Council.[17]

In February 2019, Pope Francis convoked a summit in Rome to consider the crisis of abuse. In an interview at its conclusion, Archbishop Coleridge, representing the Australian bishops, presented some of the issues clearly. He referred to the issue of abuse and its management in the Church as a 'global emergency'. He spoke of the 'need for serious cultural change', including change in the clerical culture, the education and formation for priestly ministry, greater Church transparency, greater involvement of lay people in decision-making, the way the Church speaks about its leaders, the need for structured and formal professional development for bishops, and finding better mechanisms for episcopal accountability.[18]

These appeals remind us of the humble appearance of Bishop Geoff Robinson on national television on ABC TV's 7.30 program in April 1996, where he acknowledged openly the reality of abuse in the Church, as well as his persistence in developing protocols to eradicate abuse.[19] His work, especially through his subsequent books, was welcomed by many in Australia and overseas and resisted by others in senior leadership in the Church at that time. Bishop Robinson was willing to speak openly about taboo topics – such as Rome not really 'getting it' in an ABC radio interview in the same month; the need for 'humility, honesty and compassion' in 1998;[20] and a worldwide petition that he and two other Australian bishops initiated calling on newly-elected Pope Francis to convene an ecumenical council to 'uproot' abuse by looking to its 'systemic causes'.[21]

The Royal Commission highlighted failures in two major areas: the fact and extent of abuse and the way the knowledge of abuse and offenders was handled and mis-managed. American Franciscan Joseph P. Chinnici, ofm, who, as Congregational Leader in the 1990s, was faced with knowledge of abuse by members of his order has written of his search to find an appropriate response as leader. He reflected that instances of abuse were mostly framed in interpretative systems of canon and civil law and not the context and vision of Church statements, such as *Lumen Gentium, Gaudium et Spes, Dei Verbum, Justice in the World*, or *Dignitatis Humanae*.[22] Advised in 1992 against contacting the family of victims, he lamented, 'Why must the rules of the legal forum be allowed completely to trump the truths embedded in a pastoral relationship?'[23]

Reflecting on his leadership, Chinnici called for openness of communication, collaborative strategies, a more pastoral focus and a presence to the suffering of victims, a call repeated in the LSC report which stated, that:

> ... since the People of God is first an ecclesial being, not a juridical one, its essence lies in its spirituality rather than its structures and canonical norms. The law follows and supports the theology, ecclesiology and spirituality; it does not define them.[24]

## Call for response and reform are not new

In the wake of these revelations, calls for reform of the Church from Church members have been strong and clear. Such calls for reform in Church leadership structure and practice are not new – they precede by decades the current crisis created by public knowledge of sexual abuse in the Church. There has long been a sense that the world has changed, and the Church – or many of its leaders – haven't noticed. Prior to the abuse scandals, and despite the incarnational character of our faith and despite the concept of a pilgrim Church in need of constant conversion, resistance to reform has prevailed over all the signs that the Church needed to change.

The urgency for change existed well before the shocking revelations of the Royal Commission. The decline in Church participation has been there for all to see, well before more recent statistics from the National Church Life Survey. In some areas of the Church, the climate has been inimical to openness and critique; in some, there has been a willingness to blame those who have 'left the Church' without many obvious efforts to ask why they didn't find what they needed there; in others, opportunities for healing and being heard, through close and respectful listening, seem to have been squandered. This is happening in a society where religion and church are becoming less relevant to many, as borne out by the fact that in 2016 11.8 per cent of Catholics participated actively in Church life by attending Mass regularly.[25] There is no reason to assume that attendance has increased since the 2016 Census.

There are other significant challenges. For example, that of leading a more theologically and pastorally educated faith

community: 21st century Australian parishioners are not the same as those of the 1950s, and the population in the pews at any one Mass, can be ethnically and educationally diverse. In some dioceses and institutions, there has been an apparent tendency to respond as a more corporatised Church leaving it to appear aloof and cold, concerned primarily about compliance and damage control, and prioritising a legalistic interpretation of rights and responsibilities. In other places, change has been introduced in a way which fails to respect the dignity of the women and men affected by the change.

There are particular challenges to the Church as a contemporary organisation. One example of these challenges is working with a wide range of understandings and practice in management and leadership. Another is the increasing requirements of legislation and policy regulation, administration and reporting. All such challenges create additional pressures on those in leadership roles. Those who lead ministries, while working at full capacity, are called to engage in a journey of growth as our culture undergoes significant change. At the same time, all of us in the Church, and especially those in ordained ministry, are dealing with the aftershocks of the Royal Commission, including its associated and mixed feelings of shame, guilt, anger and loss of trust.

In this context, the initiative of the Australian Bishops Conference to launch the process for a Plenary Council 2020 was mostly welcomed. The three-year process leading to the Council in 2020 has offered an invitation to all Australian Catholics to listen and contribute to future directions for the Church with its lead question, 'What is God asking of us in Australia at this present time?'[26] It is a measure of the contemporary challenge to the Church and its leadership that even the Plenary Council has been met with suspicion by some long-serving faithful members of parishes who, while entering into the process, entertain some doubts about whether their contribution will make any difference or not. The credibility of the Church's leadership to offer transparent and open communications is still being tested.[27]

It is an indicator of how urgently Catholics perceive the need for reform in their Church that the Plenary Council process has involved 222,000 participants and generated 17,457 submissions. The importance of synodality to Australian Catholics is reflected in the emergence of 'Inclusive, Participatory and Synodal?' as one of the six key themes arising from submissions and the corresponding discernment paper in preparation for the Plenary Council sessions.[28]

The seriousness with which Catholics approached the Plenary is exemplified by a group calling themselves Concerned Catholics, based in the Archdiocese of Canberra Goulburn (CCCG). Before drafting their submission, this group informed their responses through a series of forums on the Demographics of the Australian Church, Canon Law Issues, Vatican Council II, Recommendations from the Royal Commission, Church Culture and Perspectives of Pope Francis and Women, Leadership and Church. Their final submission posed five questions: 'How does the Catholic Church in Australia become and continue to be a transparent Church? An accountable Church? A non-clericalist Church?

A properly inclusive Church? A truly humble Church?' The conclusion of CCCG that 'in its current status the Australian Catholic Church is not 'fit for purpose' 'is significant given the seriousness with which this group prepared their submission. 'The characteristics of transparency, accountability, non-clericalism, inclusiveness and humility are imperatives' for the Church, they have argued, and these characteristics are 'dictated by the recommendations of the Royal Commission, the theology and ecclesiology of Pope Francis, and the deeply held faith and good sense of the Australian Catholic community'.[29]

## Leadership

Culture and leadership are at the heart of the questions posed by the Concerned Catholics of Canberra-Goulburn and echoed

by many other faithful across the country. As a lifelong advocate for leadership development Patrician Brother Aengus Kavanagh has observed, more scrutiny has focused on research relating to leadership in the past fifty years than in the previous history of civilisation up to the 1960s. This, he claims, is due to 'the universally-held conviction that leadership is the single factor that contributes more than any other to the attainment of desired results by nations, organisations, businesses, and institutions'.[30] This is as true for parishes, dioceses and Church agencies as it is for nations and other institutions.

Margaret Wheatley could well have been speaking of the Church (and the temptation in some quarters to resort to compliance and regulation) when she wrote that this chaotic world does not need bosses. What we need are leaders 'to help us develop a clear identity that lights the dark moments of confusion ... we need leaders to support us,' she continued, 'as we learn how to live by our values'. This kind of leadership will understand 'that we are best controlled by concepts that invite participation, not policies and procedures that curtail our contribution ... We all have to learn how to support the workings of each other.'[31]

Margaret Wheatley's call for leaders in society to help us to 'live by our values' recalls Vatican II's statement that the Church exercises her mission 'by the example of her life'; by walking the same road which Christ walked: 'a road of poverty and obedience, of service and self-sacrifice.'[32] Calls for a values-based leadership have been repeated in various ways by many. For example, in their 2013 petition to Pope Francis, Bishops Power, Robinson and Morris noted that many Catholics around the world were seeking change in the Catholic Church. They identified four themes they recognised in the calls from a variety of groups and places: greater inclusiveness, greater openness, greater participation and a greater sense of mission.[33] These themes were echoed in the Royal Commission and in many of the submissions to Plenary 2020.

Many good things are already happening in dioceses, parishes, schools, hospitals, aged care agencies and other ministries, which are exhibiting models of strong ecclesial leadership and leadership development. There are many agencies and structures that support the vision of a Church going forward, and the integrity and good will of those in ministries of service is palpable.

## Culture

The central hope of this book is to resource those in Church leadership to promote a change towards a more synodal culture. When Pope Francis calls for a change in culture, he is calling for deliberate action that will change the Church in a certain direction. In particular, the challenge is to move from a clericalist culture which is neither biblical, traditional nor canonical. The entanglement of clericalism in the Church's culture is deep for all in the Church, not just the ordained.

Chris Lowney, in considering the current situation of the Catholic Church, maintains that culture – 'the ways we think, operate and make decisions' – is the first thing that must change.[34] Yet while there has been a respected tradition in the Church of faithful dissenters[35], many of us have experienced how slow such change is, how hard it is to effect, and how cruel the institution can be to those whose love for the Church leads them to call for change. It appears that it is the nature of the Church itself – sacred, protective of its tradition and its own venerability – that makes cultural change so difficult.

## A brief note on 'clericalism'

The impacts of clericalism have a direct bearing on the topics covered in this book.[36] In the context of comments from the Royal Commission, the urging of Pope Francis and the aspirations of many regarding the Plenary Council, it is therefore appropriate to offer some comment on 'clericalism'.

The term is used widely and pejoratively, so in the interests of clarity and integrity, we would like to indicate some parameters. 'Clericalism' cannot be equated with clerics per se, that is, with priests or priesthood. Rather, on the individual level clericalism relates to certain behaviours, language and attitudes exhibited by some clergy – reinforced by others of the faithful – that reflect an elitist orientation, formality in relationships, and an exclusiveness that emphasises the authority of priests over other members of the faithful. One parish priest described it as an attitude of 'exception, entitlement and exemption'. Pope Francis has described clericalism as 'a really awful thing' which poses a major challenge to the Church's mission.[37]

As a culture, clericalism, in the words of Andrew Hamilton, 'displays a world view in which the Catholic Church is a self-sufficient world [a world where] its security, reputation and internal relationships are the centre of attention'.[38] Such a culture, Hamilton adds, is a culture of control that privileges secrecy. The self-sufficiency and secrecy of this clericalist culture has been lamentably demonstrated by the fact that it required a secular government to call the Church to account for its (mis)-management of child sexual abuse.

Many long-serving faithful members of the Church, both ordained and unordained, can offer instances of how they have suffered individually as a result of this culture. For example: dismissal of allegations against clergy; roughshod bypassing of normally-accepted employment practices; restricted parish life, and how the life of our Church has been diminished by its persistence (for example, in the loss of broad-based contributions to decision-making and discernment). At the same time, clericalism is far from being the full story of our Church. We must acknowledge the reality of clericalism, while at the same time honouring all those bishops, priests and other faithful who abhor it. As Hamilton again points out, 'any network of relationships is mercifully full of holes and disconnections. Even a strong clerical culture does not control everybody's behaviour.'[39]

In particular, clericalism has reduced the Church through its demeaning practices and attitudes towards women, including their exclusion from full engagement and contribution. In his reflections of seminary life in the mid-1960s, Kevin Peoples described misogyny as 'an integral part of (his) seminary training'.[40] While things have changed in the past 60 years, there is still a long way to go. Peoples quotes Bishop Robinson's insistence that 'the exclusion of women from all positions of influence in the Church has been a significant causal factor in sexual abuse …'[41] In her opening address on Case 50, Gail Furness, Senior Counsel Assisting the Royal Commission, argued that submissions to the Royal Commission strongly featured issues relating to a rigid hierarchy, based on obedience to bishops and to the Pope, with a concomitant lack of accountability to the faithful. 'The lack of women in positions of leadership was identified by many as a relevant factor.'[42]

In offering an historical correction on clericalism, John Hill emphasises that the 'ontological change' in priests with their ordination, which is often blamed for the culture of clericalism, is a misunderstanding. The special 'character' realised through the sacrament of Ordination, he explains, is parallel to that of Baptism and Eucharist, and it is essentially about the new mutual relationships between the priest and his bishop, diocese, fellow priests and other believers. It is not, he insists, about putting the clergy on any kind of pedestal. And as Vatican II reiterated in both its Decree on the Life and Ministry of Priests and the Pastoral Office of Bishops, the relationship is not one of dominance but of service.[43] So to fall back on the 'ontological change' brought through ordination as rationale for behaviours that embody a culture of clericalism is to fool oneself and to mislead others.

The behaviours, language and attitudes that reflect a culture of clericalism may well have been less remarkable in other times in history, when those in civic leadership positions also displayed similar characteristics. However, we are now in other times, times that are uncertain, complex, pluralist, and multivalent. Many of us operate simultaneously in different communities, not just one geographic-based parish society. In a world such as ours, Andrew Hamilton describes the attitudes and qualities identified with clericalism as 'both odd and counterproductive'. In such a world, he concludes, we need good leaders who 'will focus on consultation, on the claims of a common humanity and on the recognition of shared uncertainty, in order to identify the ground on which they stand and ways forward'. Such leaders who symbolise 'a humble and shared endeavour' should be encouraged – and demanded.[44]

Our final comments about clericalism take us back to our foundations. Jesus was not a cultic priest. He was a teacher who challenged the Judaic priests and entered into debate with them. He was a teacher who called women into his band of friends and disciples; at times, the Gospels report, he engaged in banter with women; one of the women who followed him – Mary from Magdala – held a responsible position in this group and became the first witness to his resurrection. He was a practising Jew who, nonetheless, chided influential pedants for imposing unfair burdens on the poor in terms of their religious observance. He did not hold himself aloof, did not wear special garb, enjoyed conviviality with all sorts. He was not, in anyone's definition, 'clericalist'.

Matthew's Gospel reports that Jesus was a leader who called his friends together, and spoke of leadership in this way:

> You know how those who exercise authority among the Gentiles lord it over them; their great ones make their importance felt. It cannot be like that with you. Anyone among you who aspires to greatness must serve the rest, and whoever wants to rank first among you must serve the needs of all. Such is the case with the Son of Man who has come, not to be served by others, but to serve, to give his own life as a ransom for the many (Matthew 20: 25-28).

## Episcopal Governance

Robert Mickens drew on the February 2019 Meeting on the Protection of Minors (the 'Abuse Summit') in Rome to illustrate that the present governing and ministerial structures of the Church are hindering the Church's mission and are 'anachronistic and inadequate to its mission and purpose'.[45] He cited the mystique surrounding the priesthood and episcopate, the imbalance in those invited to the Abuse Summit, the continued defensiveness of some Church leaders around abuse matters and the apparent inability to enforce implementation by Church leaders of guidelines, as some examples of this anachronism.

Not surprisingly, the examples given by Mickens suggest the issues of anachronism include clericalism, undue emphasis on positional authority and lack of accountability even at senior levels. Not everyone will agree with Mickens' bluntness but many faithful – at all levels in the Church's hierarchy – are echoing the call for urgent change in Church structures and governance.

## Create a new heart for me, O God[46]

Change, of course, usually comes gradually and often in a piecemeal fashion. The documents resulting from Vatican II demonstrate this in their range of ecclesiologies (not always consistent with each other) and the flow-on to contradictory understandings of leadership in the Church. This inconsistency and confusion of theologies lives on, for example, in some official Church statements advocating a greater role for parishioners in the life of the local Church, while others seemingly contradict this completely.[47] The inconsistency and confusion of theologies also lives on in language that calls for greater involvement by women in leadership in the Church while canonical structures run counter to such involvement. It is a blessing that in some situations the lived reality has not waited for these contradictions to be resolved.

This does, however, point to another critical issue for contemporary Church leadership and culture: namely a

growing polarisation into what is too-frequently caricatured as 'liberal' and 'conservative'. This is being played out at the most senior level with some Cardinals who are openly critical of Pope Francis actively engaged in undermining his papacy, and with the formalisation of 'ultra-traditionalist' groups who reject the directions coming from Vatican II. It is seen at a local diocesan level when a few clergy publicly undermine confidence in their bishop and in the sharp demarcation between different Catholic media. Terms of disparagement dishonour the members of the faithful who are so labelled, and the building of hard walls separates rather than builds up communion in our Church.

Another potential for polarisation relates to the changing demographic of Australian parishes. The impact of ethnically diverse attendees might disguise some of the decline in attendance by previously long-practising Catholics. However there is a tendency for some newly-arrived groups to bring a desire for a pietistic experience rather than for an experience of a more-engaged participative Church, as promised by Vatican II. Some priests from overseas countries similarly have brought a similar preference for piety over engagement, participation and outreach. The challenge in a Church that is truly Catholic is how to accommodate this diversity in emphasis, while still honouring the mandate endorsed by Vatican II.

A key issue in the culture of our contemporary local Church is this hunger for hospitality towards diversity. The voices of all the faithful – including the disenchanted and disappointed faithful – need to be welcomed at the table. For the God of Jesus is a father to everyone whether Indigenous or immigrant; whatever their gender, ethnicity, age, profession, sexual orientation or relationships; whatever their theological position, their spirituality and faith story. Only such generous and open-hearted hospitality will foster the dialogue, discernment, and listening to the Spirit that is necessary as we make our messy way in searching out the Kingdom Jesus spoke about.

## A broader context

This yearning for a renewed culture and revitalised leadership within the Church takes place within an exceedingly complex broader social, political and economic context. We will not elaborate on this, but simply wish to note some issues in the external environment in which the Church is called to serve at his time. Some of the factors we discern include:

- the critical reality of climate change, riddled with political leaders' inaction and polarisation, in the context of Pope Francis' call in *Laudato si'*
- the running political sore of asylum-seekers and refugees – the homeless of this world – and political paralysis in responding with compassion
- poverty, and the uneven distribution of wealth, both worldwide and in Australia, accentuated by the economic fall-out from Covid-19

- antipathy towards Church and its lack of public credibility
- lack of credibility of many national leaders and institutions – surge of populism accompanied by an apparent lack of moral compass. This spills over into a public lack of trust within the Church towards its leaders
- ongoing war and oppression
- the implications of our multicultural, plurivalent society, and
- a sense of dislocation from connection in our communities, and its associated impact on people's sense of wellbeing.

This is part of the reality in which we come together as People of God. Leaders in the communities that constitute expressions of our Church are part of this context and do not live apart from it. This context is the world in which we are called to be Church. It is our world with which we are called to dialogue; not to conquer for Christ, but in the midst of this wonderful broken world to be like Christ as we listen and hear and, in the words of John Fuellenbach, 'sniff out' the presence of God's kingdom[48], and seek to respond to the Spirit of God in furthering his Kingdom here and now.

Especially at this time of the National Plenary Council when the Australian Church is inviting the faithful to enter into dialogue about the future of our Church, in this book we share a perspective on leadership with the hope that it will build on, and build up, Church culture and leadership.

## Activity 2.1: For Reflection and Discussion

*In May 2013, Australian Bishops Morris, Power & Robinson wrote to Pope Francis. The bishops petitioned the Holy Father for a Council to address the systemic eradication of sexual abuse from the Church and noted that people around the world were calling for greater inclusiveness, openness, participation and sense of mission in the Church.*

In their submission they called for:

**Greater Inclusiveness** – a Church that is as much for women as for men, for laypeople as for clergy, for the marginalised as for those in the mainstream.

**Greater Openness** – if there are scandals, it is better to bring them into the light and confront them rather than seek to conceal them.

**Greater Participation** – not taking away the power of the Pope, but asking for greater participation and consultation, so that the whole Church may have a more active role in the mission of the Church.

**Greater Sense of Mission** – a greater concentration on the person and mission of Jesus Christ rather than on authority, laws, obedience and theological conformity.

In your own area of ministry, identify ONE area for each of these four characteristics where you have observed greater inclusiveness, openness, participation and sense of mission.

— Can you identify where the change came from?

Now, in your own area of ministry, identify ONE area that could be improved for each of these four characteristics.

— What could be done to bring about improvement in each area?

— What is blocking improvement?

— What would sustain improvement?

## Endnotes

1. The Council was in session from 11th October 1962 till 8th December 1965. It opened under the Papacy of John XXIII who died in June 1963 and was continued by his successor Pope Paul VI.
2. See Eduardo Echeverria, 'Ressourcement, Aggiornamento and Vatican II in Ecumenical Perspective,' in Homiletic and Pastoral Review, 26 July 2014, https://www.hprweb.com/2014/07/ressourcement-aggiornamento-and-vatican-ii-in-ecumenical-perspective/
3. Cf. Opening sentences, *Gaudium et Spes*, The Pastoral Constitution on the Church in the Modern World, 1965, in *Documents of Vatican II*, Geoffrey Chapman, London, 1966.
4. LG, Ch II.
5. LG, Ch VII.
6. Lennan, Mission, pp..49-50.
7. The Australian Government's *Royal Commission into Institutional Responses to Child Sexual Abuse*, April 2013-December 2017, https://www.childabuseroyalcommission.gov.au/religious-institutions, accessed 2 Dec 2019, hereafter referred to as the Royal Commission.
8. Royal Commission, *Religious Institutions*.
9. Royal Commission.
10. Royal Commission.
11. Pope Francis, *Letter to the People of God*, Preamble, 2018.
12. Pope Francis, *Letter to the People of God*, #1.
13. Bishop Vincent Long, 2018.
14. Implementation Advisory Group and Governance Review Project Team, *The Light from the Southern Cross, Promoting Co-Responsible Governance in the Catholic Church in Australia*, IAG, August 2020, hereafter referred to as LSC.
15. LSC, p. 11.
16. Due to the Covid-19 pandemic, the Plenary Council sessions were of necessity postponed twelve months to late 2021 through to mid-2022.
17. ACBC, 'Statement from Archbishop Mark Coleridge regarding the Report, Light from the Southern Cross, 12 June 2020, https://brisbanecatholic.org.au/articles/statement-by-archbishop-mark-coleridge-regarding-the-report-the-light-from-the-southern-cross/
18. Archbishop Mark Coleridge, in an interview with Joshua J. McElwee, Archbishop suggests creating a new Vatican office to tackle abuse, clerical culture, *National Catholic Reporter*, February 22, 2019, https://www.ncronline.org/print/news/accountability/exclusive-archbishop-suggests-creating-new-vatican-office-tackle-abuse-clerical
19. The 7.30 interview was 26 April 1996.
20. Geoffrey Robinson, *Confronting Power and Sex in the Church: reclaiming the Spirit of Jesus, (2008)* and *For Christ's sake, end sexual abuse in the Church ... for good* (2013) Both published by Garratt Publishing, Melbourne. See also Inform, Feb 1998.
21. Bishops Pat Power, Bill Morris, Geoffrey Robinson, Petition to Pope Francis, 2013, http://www.bishopgeoffrobinson.org/petition2013.htmLaunched in May 2013 on change.org. It attracted at least 126,281 supporters.
22. Joseph P. Chinnici ofm, *When Values collide. The Catholic Church, Sexual Abuse and the Challenges of Leadership*, Orbis Books, Maryknoll, New York, , 2010, p. 19.
23. Chinnici, p. 30.
24. LSC, p. 6.
25. National Centre for Pastoral Research, Pastoral Research Online, Issue 44, April 2019, https://ncpr.catholic.org.au/national-count-of-attendance/
26. https://plenarycouncil.catholic.org.au/pages/about-us/our-story/history/
27. For example, John Warhurst, 2019, 'Church reform must increase transparency' in Eureka St, 2nd May, and related articles
28. Plenary Council 2020, Inclusive, *Participatory and Synodal?* 2020. https://plenarycouncil.catholic.org.au/continuing-the-journey-of-discernment/
29. Concerned Catholics Canberra and Goulburn, Submission 2020 Plenary Council, 21 February 2019, https://www.concernedcatholicscanberra.org/cc-draft-submission. See also Catholics for Renewal, *Getting Back on Mission*, Garratt Publishing, Melbourne, 2019
30. Kavanagh FSP, Aengus, 'Leadership in the present context of the Catholic Church in Australia,' SWAG, Autumn, 2019
31. Wheatley, M. *Leadership and the New Science: Discovering Order in a Chaotic World*. Berrett-Koehler Publishers, San Francisco, 2006. P.131
32. AG, #5-6 in Flannery.
33. 'Petition to Pope Francis'
34. Chris Lowney, *Everyone Leads, how to revitalise the Catholic Church*, Rowman and Littlefield Publishers, Lanham, 2017, p.10
35. for example, Robert McClory, *Faithful dissenters: stories of men and women who loved and changed the church*, Orbis Books, New York, Maryknoll, 2000
36. For a useful resource on this topic, see Association of U.S. Catholic Priests, *Confronting the Systemic Dysfunction of Clericalism*, produced by the Association of U.S. Catholic Priests in collaboration with Voice of the Faithful and lay people and clergy across the nation; endorsed by FutureChurch, 2019.
37. Pope Francis, Address, Prayer Vigil with Young Italians, Rome, 11 August 2018, and Morning Meditation in the Chapel of Domus Santae Marthae, 13 December 2016.
38. Andrew Hamilton, 'Clerical culture produces poor fruit,' *Eureka Street*, 11 April 2018.
39. Hamilton, April.
40. Kevin Peoples, *Trapped in a Closed World, Catholic Culture and Sexual Abuse*, Garratt Publications, Mulgrave, 2017, p. 65.
41. Geoffrey Robinson: *For Christ's sake: end sexual abuse in the Catholic Church ... for good*, p. 72, Garratt Publishing Mulgrave, 2013, quoted by Peoples p. 66.
42. Gail Furness: 'Opening Address, Case 50', *Royal Commission into Institutional Responses to Child Sexual Abuse*, 6 February 2017, #77, https://www.childabuseroyalcommission.gov.au/case-studies/case-study-50-institutional-review-catholic-church-authorities
43. John Hill, 'Some reflections on clericalism,' in *Australasian Catholic Record* 97:2, 2020. Hill cites Vatican II, Presbyterorum Ordinis, Decree on the Ministry and Life of Priests, 7 December 1965; and *Christus Dominus*, Decree concerning the Pastoral Office of Bishops in the Church, 28 October 1965.
44. Andrew Hamilton, 'Why clericalism matters,' *Eureka Street*, 28 February 2018.
45. Robert Mickens, 'Why Catholic Church leaders risk failing on the issue of sexual abuse', *La Croix International*, 1 March 2019.
46. Cf, Psalm 51.
47. For example, *Instruction on the parish*.
48. Quoted in Lennan, *Mission*, p. 6.1

## Chapter 3
# Mission and Culture

In this chapter we will investigate 'culture' and its relationship to mission and leadership in an organisation, especially as it relates to the living out of the mission of the Church as a pilgrim Church trying to address the challenges emerging in this time of anticipated reform. These challenges have been the focus of dialogue in parishes and publications around critical issues facing the Catholic Church in Australian as it prepares for the Plenary Council. One publication lists issues of concern for a group of Catholics from Victoria[1]. While we have raised many of these earlier, the Victorian authors identify on more than 50 occasions that the source of these concerns is related to issues of 'culture', and specifically clericalism. When speaking on this issue of cultural reform, Pope Francis was specific and dramatic in describing clericalism as a perversion of the Church[2]. We personally see such cultural challenges as foundational to the mission of the Church, its leadership and its practice of its ministries.

The authors of *Getting Back on Mission* (GBOM) refer to the Royal Commission's comment that the culture of clericalism has corrupted Church governance. Good governance, they state, is driven by the character and values of people and processes which go beyond structure, power and rules. Ultimately it is 'an organisation's leadership and culture [that)] will determine the efficacy of its governance, even with sound structures and practices in place.'[3]

This chapter will investigate the nature and elements of culture, why it is so powerful in effecting outcomes for people and institutions, and why it plays such a foundational role in the life of organisations such as the Catholic Church.

## The nature of culture

We see culture broadly as the glue that holds individuals and groups together. 'Culture' has known many definitions, with a particularly helpful insight being offered by Van Maanen who suggests that culture looks at the essence of values and beliefs, the expression of needs, the purposes, hopes, and desires of people, and the meanings and significances that provides deep sources of satisfaction in groups and institutions in which they live. These become a set of shared understandings, interpretations or perspectives that enable people to communicate appropriately within the context of their group.[4] Edgar Schein adds a slightly different perspective, emphasising the overt and covert nature of culture:

> Perhaps the most intriguing aspect of culture as a concept is that it points us to phenomena that are below the surface, that are powerful in their impact but invisible and to a considerable degree unconscious. In that sense, culture is to a group what personality or character is to an individual.[5]

Schein also stresses that culture is built around shared values, beliefs and assumptions about the mission, values and purpose of an organisation and how people behave in everyday life within the organisation, or 'the way people do things around here' and why. In this way, culture is seen as a pattern of shared assumptions that a group has learned while solving its problems of external adaptation and internal integration in a way satisfactory enough to be considered valid, and therefore to be taught to new members as the correct way to perceive, think and feel in relation to moral problems.[6] People learn how to survive, fail or thrive through absorbing culture by observing the traits, mores, traditions, languages, behaviour, passions, procedures, loves and hates of the people sharing their place. We learn how to be one of these people by understanding what is important and insignificant in our lives. Culture is the window to the heart and character of the institution.

The concept of culture as an iceberg can be used to illustrate that there are visible and invisible characteristics of culture, the majority of which are hidden to the observer, and that mission and organisational values lie in this submerged part of the culture.[7] Like an iceberg, nine out of ten manifestations of culture are unseen. The surface level is overt, where more observable elements reside, such as buildings, uniforms, infrastructure, policies and procedures, services and products, financial resources and stated mission and goals. The submerged and covert components are where the actual beliefs, assumptions, values and feelings about how the place operates both formally and informally, reside. It is further suggested that the manifestations of culture are experienced at three levels, surface, shallow and deep. More significantly,

the emotional levels concerning these elements are seen to increase with depth. Errors of dress or language may provoke mild rebuke, possibly even through humour, but offence to the professional mission of members or evidence of unethical behaviour in the pursuit of the values and mission of the institution could meet with stern disapproval, even expulsion from the group.

These three levels give insights to how cultures can become counter-productive: level 1 is what we see, level 2 are the espoused values of the organisation, and level 3 the underlying assumptions about what is really valued.[8] Cultures that become dysfunctional usually do so because of the misalignment of values at these three levels. An organisation may claim in its mission statement that its priority is the interests of its customers or clients. As such, staff are taught customer and client service. If the experience of members is that profits or accountability to costs is more important than service, that is the assumption and value that gets learned and prized. When organisations consistently breach stated and assumed mission values it is possible that some deeper, unwritten beliefs are in operation. Such was the message from the 2019 report of the Banking Royal Commission in Australia where banks and financial institutions admitted to violating their stated missions of customer service. They did this by charging dead clients for services that were clearly never delivered. Philip Pogson criticises the hypocrisy of an organisation that touts openness as one of its values, while regularly doing everything to block customers and regulators from gaining access to freely available data. He states that such behaviour creates the tacit assumption for staff that their role is to act to protect the reputation of the organisation at any cost. Pogson concluded,

> Strange that it took a royal commission into institutional child abuse to bring to light the fact that many in leadership roles in some of our most respected organisations considered the good reputation of their institution to be more important than the welfare of the children they cared for.[9]

There are different tools that can be used to attempt to assess and understand an organisation's culture. One such tool assesses an organisation's culture by observing certain characteristics which, expressed here in general organisational terms, relate directly to the focus of various sections of our text, as shown:

1. Member identity: the degree to which members identify and own the organisation as a whole (see Chapter 1).

2. Group emphasis: the degree to which activities are organised around groups rather than individuals (see Chapter 4).

3. People focus: the degree to which decisions, at all levels, take into consideration the effect of outcomes on people and involve them in decisions affecting them within the organisation (see Chapters 5, 6, 8 and 9).

4. Unit integration: the degree to which units within the organisation are encouraged to operate in a coordinated or interdependent manner (see Chapter 6).

5. Control: the degree to which rules, regulations & direct supervision are used to oversee and control behaviour (see Chapter 7).

6. Risk tolerance: the degree to which leaders are encouraged to be aggressive, innovative and risk-seeking (see Chapter 8).

7. Reward criteria: the degree to which rewards such as salary increases and promotions are allocated on performance criteria in contrast to seniority, favouritism or other non-performance factors (see Chapters 7 and 9).

8. Conflict tolerance: the degree to which members are encouraged to air conflicts and criticisms openly (see Chapter 4 and 9).

9. Means-end orientation: the degree to which leaders focus on results or outcomes rather than on techniques and processes used to achieve those outcomes (see Chapter 5 and 9).

10. Open systems focus: the degree to which the organisation monitors and responds to changes in the external environment[10] (see Chapter 6 and Chapter 8).

The mission and values of groups and institutions will affect these characteristics, define the culture, and give it a character and personality that is distinctive from that of another organisation with a different mission. Significantly, for our analysis of the culture of the Church, the living out of those beliefs and values that we have described as the mission of the Church gives meaning to the life of the organisation and its members and determines its ultimate success. This understanding puts the words of Pope Francis and the Royal Commission about the culture of the Church, especially as it relates to the dysfunctional and misalignment effects of clericalism, into stark relief.

## Culture and mission

A mission statement for any organisation is usually a brief description of the business it carries out and the means for achieving its purpose across a wide range of situations. It attempts to describe succinctly what would result from the achievement of the institution when operating at its best.[11]

Earlier we discussed the core mission of the Church and identified challenges resulting from a disconnect between this mission (what is believed, valued and cherished about being members of the faithful), and what has been identified as shortcomings occurring in the life of the Church. As we have discussed, a mission is essentially individuals committing to values that are shared in communion with others. It is easy, then, to see the reason for the passion, fear, and sometimes anger, expressed by Church groups seeking reform in the personal ownership of the values that give the mission its validity. The issue of cultural reform in the Church can be viewed in this context as values in contest. The significance of this rests in the ways people experience values in their lives. There are many different definitions of the nature of values. The following are examples of the most commonly accepted definitions:

> **Example 1:** Values are the importance or worth that an individual attaches to particular activities or objects or an outcome[12] (such as salvation, caring or belonging).
>
> **Example 2:** Values can be personal cognitive standards as to what should be desired, what is important and cherished, and what standards of conduct or existence are personally or socially acceptable[13] (such as humility, compassion, respect).
>
> **Example 3:** Values can be an enduring belief that a specific mode of conduct or end-state of existence is personally or socially preferable to an opposite or converse mode of conduct or end-state of existence[14] (such as salvation/damnation, forgiveness/retribution, peace/war).

Mission is a valuation process that is owned at the individual and group level. It takes its power from the strength and authenticity with which values are held by its adherents. Not only do our values direct our behaviour, they also help us make judgements about other people's beliefs based on what is assumed about them from observation and understandings of their behaviour. In this context, a challenge facing the Church anytime, including during the Australian Plenary Council, is to discern the faithfulness of the structure and processes of the Church to its mission.

The cultural mission of religious organisations such as hospitals, schools, homes and dioceses will reflect both the wider norms and behaviours inherent within the organisation and general society in which it operates, and reflect the more specific values associated with the mission of the organisation. Helping and serving organisations like those established for social welfare or healthcare reasons, have different cultural characteristics and purposes from those established as commercial profit-making concerns. This is primarily due to their core mission of social good. The clash of values inherent in these cultures is evidenced daily in the lives of service leaders as they battle for the maintenance of their professional missions of service, health or care against the legitimate demands for financial and resource accountability, professional accountability and responsibility to funding sponsors.

Religious organisations will experience the same professional and accountability tensions as their secular equivalents. However, cultural tensions in Church institutions are further complicated by their endeavour to further their religious mission and the values that it represents, in a modern, secular and materialistic society, where these values may not be, or seem to be, of great interest. For this reason, churches and their institutions, especially schools, are sometimes seen as counter-cultural as their mission and culture often contradict and contest the values of the general community in which they live and serve.

While the evangelical role of the Church's mission commits it to such critique and contest, its success will clearly rest on the strength of its mission and culture to exert influence over local, national, or global cultures in which it operates.[15] Creating strong mission-focused cultures has been a challenge for millennia; the challenge now, while different, is profound, not just for the external influence of the Church but for its internal survival.

The mission of the Church, built on a special mission of discipleship, requires a culture that demonstrates and celebrates values consistent with this mission. Without this consistency, there will be a disconnect and misalignment of values between mission and reality, a situation clearly considered by Catholics for Renewal.[16]

## Cultural leadership

Schein, whose work we discussed earlier, places the responsibility for the creation of authentic and living cultures squarely in the hands of leaders. He claims:

> One could argue that the only thing of real importance that leaders do is to create and manage culture, and that the unique talent of leaders is their ability to understand and work with culture. If one

wishes to distinguish leadership from management or administration one can argue that leaders create and change cultures, while managers and administrators live with them.[17]

Others have extended this important cultural role of leaders to the need for them to seek clarity about their values and convictions[18] as those who do are better able to resist social or situational pressures to compromise their values[19]. 'Good leaders', it has been said, 'are perceived by others as being aware of their own and others' values, knowledge, and strengths; aware of the context in which they operate; and who are confident, hopeful, optimistic, resilient, and high on moral character.'[20]

If culture determines 'the way we do things around here,' then it is essential that the leader ensures that the culture experience is aligned with mission values. If the mission is reflected in cultural values, then alignment cannot be left to chance because it can be contested by individual and organisational self-interest and misplaced assumptions about purpose. When analysing the importance of cultural leadership, Thomas Greenfield challenged the use of management paradigms in building cultures and pointed instead to the importance of values and morality, maintaining that 'the task of leadership is to create the moral order that binds them (leaders) and the people around them'.[21]

The following diagram by Branson (Figure 3.2) shows the expanding elements of cultural alignment as rings in a concentric circle. The centre represents the mission of an organisation. This core is a collaboratively discerned controlling insight about what followers value, what they are striving to achieve and what is necessary for the survival and growth of that organisation. This core is driven by the interior values and lives of the organisational members, especially its leaders. (How these core interior values influence this mission and the culture will be addressed later.) The elements shown in the succeeding rings add detail to the mission by showing how its success will be experienced, how the values and beliefs are stated and celebrated, how members feel about their membership of the organisation, and how outcomes are owned and prized. It asserts that clarifying and developing guiding beliefs about operational values benefits stakeholders by contributing to their understanding of the significance of their contributions, which can influence their morale and the overall success of the institution.[22]

The central values of the mission at the heart of the model are crucially influenced by the interior life and values of the leader. The model also suggests that understanding what success would look like, institutionally and individually, and how that success reflects the specific mission values, provides motivation and commitment for stakeholders to be engaged and contribute fully to the achievement of the mission. Part of the assumptions regarding the building of strong cultures through the application of such evolving detail is that the establishment of such characteristics tests

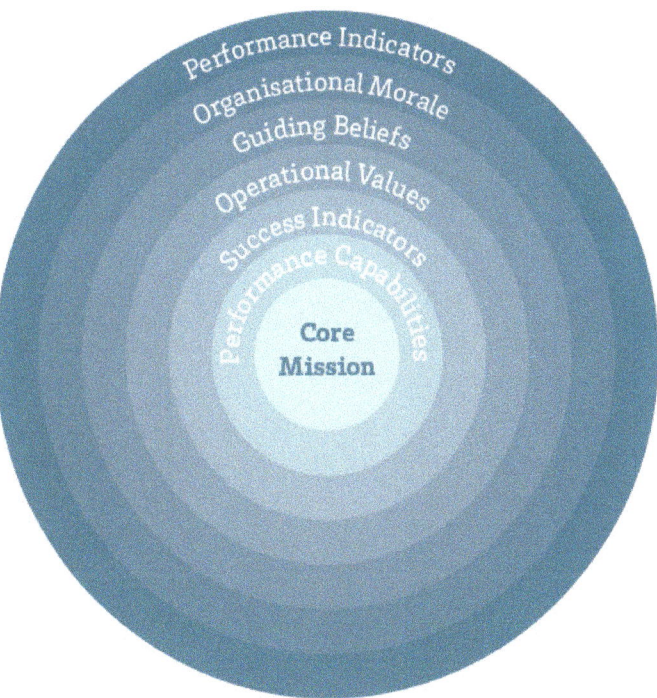

Figure 3.1 Values Alignment Model

the capabilities of the organisation to meet the goals of the mission. This is achieved through identifying the strengths and weaknesses and specific behaviours of the culture of the organisation at varying levels, including groups and individuals.

The model suggests that dialogue about these crucial ingredients enables the group to better reinforce the strengths or overcome weaknesses in these categories. This is done through specifically targeting group and individual change processes. The Plenary Council is a means of such a renewal and change process and its major performance indicator will be the universal discernment and strengthening of the mission of the Catholic Church in Australia. In regard to the Plenary, it should be understood that mission only becomes powerful it is from within that the people involved both see the forces shaping them, and discern how they may play a part in the evolution of a new reality.[23]

Practically, these forces of renewal initially rest in the hands of leaders who can achieve essential cultural alignment by attending to mechanisms in their organisation. Mechanisms for embedding aligned cultures can include actions, such as how leaders:

a. pay attention to, measure, and assess culture on a regular basis

b. react to critical incidents of cultural misalignment

c. allocate resources

d. deliberately role model and coach others,

e. allocate rewards and status

f. recruit, select, or terminate members.

Mechanisms for reinforcing culture can include elements, such as:

a. community design and structure

b. community systems and procedures

c. rites, rituals and ceremonies of the community

d. design of physical space, facades, and buildings

e. stories about important events and people

f. formal statements of a community's philosophy, creeds, and charters.[24]

While these cultural mechanisms create an important framework by which leaders can influence and change their organisation's culture, the character and characteristics of the leader will also have a major influence on the outcome of these mechanisms towards building strong cultures. These cultural leadership characteristics can emerge best from accurate knowledge of self, and leaders' values, and beliefs about what is moral and ethical in their calling to serve a community. Later we will investigate moral discernment and decision-making for leaders that will extend these positions.

## The interior life of the cultural leader

Other personal and social perspectives that will influence the type of culture that leaders create include their personal characteristics, such as their emotional and social intelligence.[25] These intelligences incorporate approaches to power, influence, responsibility and authority in relationships with people and community, and also beliefs about what motivates, connects and commits people to groups and organisations. Goleman sees self-awareness as crucial to being able to self-regulate, show empathy and care for others.[26] His perspective suggests we must first know ourselves if we are to be able to be responsible for our actions with others; and unless we have that foundation of self-understanding, empathy and social skills will be superficial and fall away under the pressure of leadership.

Understanding why one wants to lead and the motivations for this desire will be crucial to questions about serving others and sharing power and influence. If the leader is ambitious for promotion for personal satisfaction and gain, the culture developed will reflect this self-interest in a lack of ownership, trust and authenticity among the community. Empathy for reasons of self-benefit will be viewed as manipulation by others in the relationship and doom the development of trust and commitment. How personal awareness and emotional intelligence are developed are complex and challenging elements in leadership development. We will touch on this issue later when we deal with developing leadership for a synodal Church.

How leaders view power, influence and authority are also important elements in the culture they develop. French philosopher Michel Foucault has cautioned aspirants to leadership roles to be aware that power gives influence but that it does not rest with them as individuals, nor in their various characteristics, nor in the position to which they

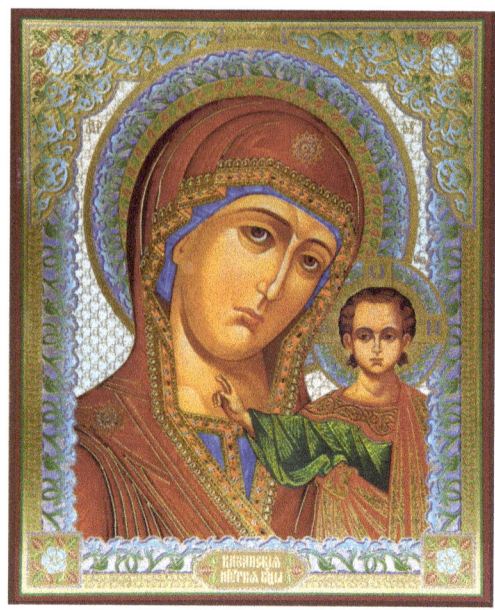

aspire. Rather, power rests in the relationship with the people who are being served, especially with those perceived to have less power and influence in the organisation. He also sees true power resting in the character of the organisation – its truth, openness, honesty and fairness and its sense of purpose being driven by shared purpose.[27] This view of power and how others are influenced in organisations again stresses the importance of values alignment and truth to mission. For this reason, we will explore these approaches to relational leadership further, especially through the transrelational approach to leadership developed by Branson and associates. Stressing that people 'now want their leaders to be relationally adept rather than predominantly technically accomplished', Branson et al describe the important fundamentals of cultural leadership as being 'relationships, interpersonal skills, collegiality, cooperation and teamwork' and states that these are far more essential to the practice of leadership 'than a continuing commitment to meeting predetermined goals, externally defined accountability, individual self-interests and personal ambitions'.[28]

## Conclusion

This chapter has analysed the concept of culture, and indicated that both academic literature and Church reform groups have identified a healthy culture as crucial to any change that may result from reform processes such as the Plenary Council. The links of culture to mission were stressed as was the importance of leadership to effective cultures. The characteristics and actions of cultural leadership have been addressed, and these elements will be complemented in a broader review of leadership offered in Chapter 5. In the following chapters we will analyse the implications of having a culture aligned to our faith and mission through the creation of a synodal Church, especially as expressed in the areas of governance, leadership, people, moral decision-making, training and development.

# Activity 3.1: What are my values?

*List those values which you firmly believe are regularly influencing your behaviour. How many did you list? Provide a practical example of how each value has influenced your behaviour, especially in your attitudes towards leadership. If you are comfortable about sharing these insights, discuss with a trusted colleague and explore how they view your insights.*

# Activity 3.2: Possible assumptions regarding leadership arising from misalignments of mission values and culture in the Church

Some submissions to the Royal Commission into Institutional Responses to Child Sexual Abuse have been interpreted as possible evidence of tacit assumptions of senior Church and institutional leaders that:

- Unordained people cannot be trusted to play a significant role in the leadership of the Church.
- Protecting the reputation of the Church is one of its leadership's key tasks.
- Transparency in decision-making and governance will be used as a weapon against Church leaders, particularly by a hostile media.

Taking the fact that Diocesan Pastoral Councils and Parish Pastoral Councils are not yet universally established in the Australian Church, reflect and discuss possible assumptions that might explain this misalignment between the stated values of the Church, and its practice, in light of the discussion in the text about levels of culture. For example:

- The lack of formal training in theology of many parishioners is seen as a barrier to their playing a significant role in pastoral discernment at a parish or diocesan level.
- The faithful are not regarded as having the moral right to make decisions within the parish or diocese.
- An individual parish or diocesan leader can ignore the counsels of the Church and obstruct the involvement of the faithful if it doesn't suit them personally.

# Activity 3.3: Building your leadership credo

1. Reflect on one of the values you identified in the earlier activity or a value that you hold about being a leader in a Catholic context.

2. Following the model presented on page 30, list the beliefs you hold about this value.

3. Try to give these beliefs a number (e.g. for value one there are five beliefs 1.1-1.5).

4. Try not to use the words of the value in the statements of the beliefs and try to write full sentences about the beliefs.

5. Under 'ideology' write the things we ought and ought not see, hear, do, feel, if we were 'meeting' these beliefs.

6. Finally, record methods by which we could indicate our success in meeting these values and beliefs.

7. Carry out this activity yourself, then share the result with a colleague. If a member of a staff, board or team, share the material with the group and discuss what you have learned from reading the Credo of a peer.

8. Does this activity suggest the team should spend time in dialogue about shared or contested values that may be held and which could affect the department, board, parish, school or ministry team?

## Leadership Belief Model

Value: Choose one Leadership Value at a time to work through the following. (Examples of values are Trust, Authenticity, Caring, Competence, Authority, Faith, Spirituality.)

| Beliefs | Ideology | | Evidence |
|---|---|---|---|
| What are your beliefs about this value? | What things ought we see, hear, do and feel if we were meeting these beliefs? | What things ought we not see, hear, do and feel if we were meeting these beliefs? | What will you accept as proof that this value is present in you, the institution or the community? |
| Belief 1. | 1. | 1. | 1. |
|  | 2. | 2. | 2. |
|  | 3. | 3. | 3. |
| Belief 2. | 1. | 1. | 1. |
|  | 2. | 2. | 2. |
|  | 3. | 3. | 3. |

## Endnotes

1. See Catholics for Renewal, *Getting back on Mission*, (GBOM), Garratt Publishing, Melbourne, 2019.
2. Pope Francis, Address, Prayer Vigil with Young Italians, Rome, 11 August 2018 and Morning Meditation in the Chapel of Domus Santae Marthae, 13th December 2016.
3. *GBOM*, p. 127.
4. J. Van Maanen, *Tales of the field: On writing ethnography* (2nd ed.), The University of Chicago Press, 2011.
5. E. H. Schein, *Organizational culture and leadership* (Vol. 2), John Wiley & Sons, New York, 2010, p. 8. http://ezproxy.acu.edu.au/login?url=http://site.ebrary.com/lib/australiancathu/detail.action?docID=1 0418988
6. E. H. Schein, 'The role of the founder in creating organizational culture', *Organizational Dynamics*, 12:1, 1983. Retrieved from http://www.elsevier.com/locate/org
7. T. Rick, *Organisational culture is like an iceberg*, www.torbenrick.eu/blog/culture/organizational-culture-is-like-an-iceberg/
8. See Schein, 2010.
9. P. Pogson, *When organisations trash their own values-and why we should care*, linked in 23/08/20.
10. S. Robbins, & D. De Cenzo, *Fundamentals of Management*, 4th Edition, Pearson, 2004.
11. D. J. Willower, 'Philosophy and the study of educational administration.' *The Journal of Educational Administration*, 23:1, 1985, pp. 5-22.
12. D. Gerber, *Toward an Anthropological Theory of Value: The False Coin of Our Own Dreams*. Palgrave, New York, 2001.
13. B. Posner & R.Westwood, An international perspective on shared values, paper presented to Annual Meeting of the Academy of International Business, Maui, Hawaii, October, 1993.
14. M. Rokeach, *The Nature of Values*, Free Press, 1973, p. 5.
15. See M. J. Wheatley, *So far from home. Lost and found in our brave new world*. Berrett-Koehler Publishers, San Francisco, 2012.
16. See Catholics for Renewal, *Getting back on Mission*, (GBOM) Garratt Publishing, Melbourne, 2019.
17. Schein, p. 5.
18. B. Shamir & G. Eilam, 'What's Your Story?' A Life-Stories Approach to Authentic Leadership Development.' *The Leadership Quarterly*, 16, 2005. pp. 395-417.
19. See Erik Erikson, *Dimensions of a New Identity. Jefferson Lectures in the Humanities*. W. W. Norton & Co, New York. 1974.
20. B. Avolio, B. O. Walumbra & T.J. Weber, 'Leadership, Current Theories, Research, and Future Directions,' Annual Review of Psychology, 60, 2009, pp. 421-449.
21. T.B. Greenfield, Leaders and Schools: Willfulness and Non-Natural Order in Organisation, in *Leadership and Organisational Culture*, edited by T. Sergiovanni & J. Corbally, University of Illinois Press, 1984, p. 570.
22. C. Branson, *Leadership for an Age of Wisdom*, Springer Educational Publishing, Dordrecht, 2009.
23. P. M. Senge, C. O. Scharmer, J. Jaworski & B. S. Flowers, 'Awakening faith in an alternative future,' *Reflections*, 5:7, 2004, pp.1-11.
24. C. M. Branson, Community Formation Module 2, EDLE 681, Australian Catholic University, 2016.
25. See D. Goleman, *Emotional intelligence*, Bantam Books, 2006.
26. Goleman.
27. Michel Foucault, *The Subject and Power*, University of Chicago Press, 1982.
28. Branson et al, 2019, p. 4.

# Chapter 4
# The Culture of a Synodal Church

Pope Francis' vision for a change in Church culture and life is well-publicised. The changes he calls for embrace, among other things, conversion, deep spirituality, an end to clericalism and a strengthening of what he calls 'synodality', all of which are interrelated within the Church's culture. Synodality embraces something much richer than simply a culture of greater consultation and dialogue. In this chapter, we will explore its origins and what it could mean for the culture of our Church.

Synods as formal institutions in the recent Church are associated with Pope Paul VI. In response to Vatican II, and because of 'esteem and regard for all the Catholic bishops and with the aim of providing them with abundant means for greater and more effective participation in our concern for the universal Church', Pope Paul instituted the Synod of Bishops as an ongoing forum where representative bishops from around the world could advise him from time to time on particular issues.[1] Since then there have been 15 General Synods;[2] three Extraordinary Synods; and 11 Special Synods held in different regions of the world.[3]

The Constitution on the Church that resulted from Vatican II expressed this communion in terms of collegiality, 'the Successor of Peter governing the Church in collaboration with, and the participation of, the bishops of the local Churches, respecting their joint responsibility for the Universal Church'. Within Chapter III of the Constitution (The Hierarchical Structure), 'synodality is one particular expression of that rightful participation of the local Churches in governance, through consultation'.[4]

Pope Francis continues to emphasise the priority of synodality in his papacy, extending the principle beyond episcopal synods. 'From the beginning of my ministry as Bishop of Rome', he wrote in 2015 on the occasion of the 50th anniversary of Pope Paul VI's institution of the Synod of Bishops, 'I sought to enhance the Synod, which is one of the most precious legacies

of the Second Vatican Council.' Pope Francis went on to say that Pope Paul had foreseen that the organisation of the Synod could 'be improved upon with the passing of time' and both Saint John Paul II and Benedict XVI had sought to do so.[5] Pope Francis is speaking about complementing the spirit of collaboration and collegiality of the Synod of Bishops with processes of discernment in the Church that include all the members.

Pope Francis' ardent commitment to a wider sense of participation and dialogue about synodality is unambiguous. In regard to the way in which the Church needs to discern its way forward, Francis writes that 'we must continue along this path. The world in which we live, and which we are called to love and serve, even with its contradictions, demands that the Church strengthen cooperation in all areas of her mission'. And he adds that it is 'precisely this path of synodality which God expects of the Church of the third millennium'.[6] His language is compelling: this is what God expects of us.

As always, as we have come to expect with Pope Francis, he brings a spiritual challenge to this concept: far from urging the Church to become a democracy, he is asserting the need for a 'holy union of energies in the service of the common good of the Church', as Vatican II described the goal of bishops working in synod.[7] In the words of the International Theological Commission, synodality '... should not be understood in the sense of conciliarism on the ecclesiological level or of parliamentarianism on a political level. It is more helpful to think in terms of exercising synodality at the heart of ecclesial communion.'[8] Pope Francis typically put it more simply when he said synodality is 'the presence of the Holy Spirit, otherwise it is not synodality, it is a parlour, a parliament, something else'.[9]

At the conclusion of the 2018 Synod on Youth, the Pope wrote: 'It is in relationships – with Christ, with others, in the community – that faith is handed on.' In the same way, Pope Francis continued, the Church is called to 'adopt a relational manner', for the sake of its mission. Such a relational approach 'places emphasis on listening, welcoming, dialogue and common discernment in a process that transforms the lives of those taking part'.[10]

It can certainly be transforming to be listened to without judgement; to be given the rare gift of someone else's focused attention. This is the kind of listening that Pope Francis describes when he speaks of a listening Church that knows 'listening' is more than 'hearing'. It is, he says, 'a mutual listening in which everyone has something to learn. The faithful people, the college of bishops, the Bishop of Rome: all listening to each other, and all listening to the Holy Spirit, the Spirit of truth in order to know what he says to the Churches.' Then he adds something very significant. This is not just one aspect of the Church: it is a 'constitutive element' of the Church.[11]

In reading these words of Pope Francis about learning together, we were reminded of a national conference of Catholic educators we attended in New Zealand some years ago. Every New Zealand bishop attended the entire conference, but not only for the keynote addresses, liturgies and formal celebrations. In itself, this was affirming for the country's Catholic school leaders and teachers. More significantly, the bishops attended as full participants, joining in workshops, asking questions, listening to teachers and learning with them.

## Synodality is essential to being Church

In making synodality a priority, Pope Francis is drawing on some of the oldest traditions of the Church when the early Christians met as a community as portrayed in the *Acts of the Apostles*.[12] With community and friendship often going hand in hand, Joseph Lam has suggested that the notion of friendship could be seen to underlie synodality and leadership, heightening as it does, 'attention to the "togetherness" of the journey'. He proposes how in Acts 2:41-47 Luke, who wrote for a Hellenistic audience, described the typical hospitality of friendship valued in Greco-Roman culture where a shared meal was seen as 'the most suitable occasion to live the central aspects of friendship, such as intimacy, common vision and equality'. In contributing to the cost of the friendship meal, the group demonstrated their equality and homogeneity. Lam concludes that the members of the first community were not just disciples, but believers and believers' friends.[13]

The early Christians gathered under the leadership of the Holy Spirit as they discerned how they were to live faithful to their experience of Jesus.[14] Acts is filled with references to the early Christians moving under the stirring of the Spirit. For example Paul was 'compelled by the Spirit' to set forth for Jerusalem, not knowing what would happen to him there.[15] It was in community – synodality – that the early Church responded to the complaint that some widows were being overlooked. The Twelve gathered all the disciples together and asked them to choose seven wise and spirit-filled disciples from the group to minister to those in need in the community.[16]

The prime example of synodality in action often quoted by theologians occurred around 48CE when the early Christians sought to discern whether or not non-Jewish converts should be circumcised. Acts 15:1-4 reports how Christians in Antioch had been distressed by some visitors from Jerusalem who had insisted that non-Jewish believers should be circumcised. We can imagine the emotional turmoil in the community at Antioch summed up in the reference to 'no small dissension and debate' (Acts 15:2). So the community of Gentiles sent Paul and Barnabas to Jerusalem to sort out the matter. 'When they came to Jerusalem,' we read, 'they were welcomed by the church and the apostles and elders, to whom they reported everything God had done through them' (Acts 15:4). There the question of circumcision was discussed in a forum composed of apostles and elders with the final decision taken by the whole assembly.[17] This would occur with much debate – a reminder that dialogue is often messy.

If we apply the language of Robins and Decenzo, we can describe the synodal Apostolic Church as having a tolerance for conflict, and not hesitating to face up to dissonance and diversity of views. From the beginning, dialogue was a key to resolving disputes. Following the resolution of the circumcision issue, the 'apostles and the elders, with the consent of the whole Church', wrote to the community in Antioch in a way which gives a profound insight into their understanding of the process they had just been through. Their words state that '... it has seemed good to the holy Spirit and to us...'[18] 'The holy Spirit and us' is a powerful phrase of alliance.

The outcome of this synodal discernment was to observe the principle of imposing on the Gentile Christians no more burden than was necessary, no requirements other than those essential to Christian belief. Further, the church in Jerusalem sent additional messengers to encourage the people in Antioch in person. In response, the community there was heartened and became stronger (Acts 15:28-35).

The International Theological Commission (ITC) comments that the means of discernment used in Jerusalem involved everyone in the Church listening to the holy Spirit, with each person giving his/her own judgment, so that, through community dialogue, initially divergent opinions reached a consensus and unanimity that served the evangelising mission of the Church. And the ITC adds in an inspirational summary,

> ... all are equally responsible for the life and mission of the community and all are called to work in accordance with the law of mutual solidarity in respect of their specific ministries and charisms, inasmuch as every one of them finds his or her energy in the one Lord (cf. 1 Corinthians 15:45).[19]

In short, synodality has a long history and from the beginning was an integral element of being Church, with the early Christians discerning under the guidance of the holy Spirit with a focus on the mission of Jesus. This character of being Church continued well into the Church's history till around the 14th Century. In the medieval Church a principle of Roman law was used: *Quod omnes tangit, ab omnibus tractari et approbari debet* – 'what affects everyone, should be discussed and approved by all'.[20] It has only been in the centuries since then that a more hierarchical Rome-centred approach to discernment by the Church has held sway.[21]

In 1972, just a few years after Vatican II, German theologian Rudolf Schnackenburg asked, 'How can lay people (the majority of the people of God) share, in full responsibility, in the decisions of the Church?' Acknowledging that Church organisation had become more formalised with an increasing emphasis on the episcopate, he insists that 'the cooperation and co-responsibility of the whole community, so prominent in New Testament times, were indispensable elements in the life of the Church which must be taken even more seriously into account today'.[22]

In 1968, Cardinal Suenens of Belgium, who had participated in Vatican II, commented that, 'History will render glory to the council for having beautifully defined the nature of the Church, the people of God, and for having boldly sketched the place and the role of the laity in the Church.' He then added, 'History will no doubt also accuse us of not having sufficiently put into practice that which is so well defined – the co-responsibility of the laity.'[23] Were he still alive, it would be interesting to hear Cardinal Suenens' reflection on recent developments in the practice of co-responsibility in the Church.

## Synodality, revelation and *sensus fidei*

The foundations for Pope Francis' emphasis on synodality were laid in Vatican II with its focus on two insights in particular: (i) all baptised as the People of God, and (ii) a new understanding of revelation. Myriam Wijlens explains how Vatican II's Constitution on Revelation[24] shifted the understanding from a hierarchical transmission of the faith to a clarification that 'revelation occurs within the whole people of God' and that

from this the Council drew an extremely important conclusion, that the believing Church – *in credendo* – is infallible.[25] The Spirit of God works through the community.

From this it follows that an essential element of synodality is the *sensus fidei* of the Church.[26] *Sensus fidei* recognises that, through Baptism, all the faithful are anointed by the holy Spirit and so share in the prophetic role of Jesus himself.[27] *Sensus fidei* includes two aspects: (i) a 'sense for the faith' given by the Spirit to each baptised believer and (ii) the faith held within the People of God as a whole.[28]

In the first, *sensus fidei* refers to each individual believer as being under the guidance of the Spirit whereby '... the gifts of the Spirit confer a faculty of perceiving the truth of the faith and of discerning anything opposed to it.'[29] It recognises that '... the faithful have an instinct for the truth of the gospel, which enables them to recognise and endorse authentic Christian doctrine and practice, and to reject what is false.' At this personal level, *sensus fidei* enables an individual believer: a) to discern the authenticity to faith of a particular teaching or practice; b) to distinguish between the essential and the secondary in what is preached, and c) to discern the witness to Jesus Christ that they should give in their particular time and circumstances.[30] *Sensus fidei* is the Spirit's instrument for interpreting divine revelation.

The second aspect, *sensus fidelium*, pertains to the faith held by the Church as a whole. Vatican II emphasised the importance of *sensus fidelium*, stating in the Constitution on the Church, that 'the body of the faithful as a whole, anointed as they are by the Holy One cannot err in matters of belief'.[31] As Myriam Wijlens comments,

> The *sensus fidelium* finds its most comprehensive and at the same time most diverse expression in the lived faith ... The (Second Vatican) Council draws an extremely important conclusion from this: she affirms that the Church in *credendo* – the believing Church – is infallible.[32]

In an interview in 2013, Pope Francis expressed the *sensus fidelium* in terms of the faithful, considered as the whole Church, being infallible in matters of beliefs. The people, he wrote, 'display this *infallibilitas in credendo*, this infallibility in believing, through a supernatural sense of the faith of all the people walking together. *Sentire cum Ecclesia* [to think and to feel with the Church] is my way of being a part of this people.'[33]

The convergence of the individual believer's *sensus fidei* and whole-of-Church *sensus fidelium* is made possible when the magisterium of the Church listens to the faithful. The ITC states that the Church's teaching authority, as expressed by the Pope and Bishops, must listen to the *sensus fidelium*, or what the ITC calls 'the living voice of the people of God'. Not only do the People of God 'have the right to be heard', the Theological Commission continues, but their response to what is proposed as part of the faith handed down from the Apostles 'must be taken very seriously, because it is by the Church as a whole that the apostolic faith is borne in the power of the Spirit. The magisterium does not have sole responsibility for it'.[34] This is where synodality becomes not only helpful, but necessary, providing spaces where this listening and hearing can occur.

In summary, the *sensus fidei fidelis* is a 'sort of spiritual instinct that enables the (individual) believer to judge spontaneously whether a particular teaching or practice is or is not in conformity with the Gospel and with apostolic faith'.[35] Through the exercise of *sensus fidei*, lay members of the Church have actively contributed to shaping the development of the belief of the whole Church.[36] *Sensus fidei* is not a matter of public opinion. It is not a poll, a voting for and against any given issue or topic. It is about reflecting in faith, open to the Spirit, in response to Jesus Christ. It is not about majority opinions, nor has it been that way in the history of God's people, the beginning of Christianity itself and throughout Church history.[37] Certain dispositions are required for authentic participation in the *sensus fidei*. Since it is an exercise in faith, and for faith, it presumes faithfulness in those exercising their prophetic role in this way. The ITC identifies these as:

a) participation in the life of the Church,
b) listening to the word of God,
c) openness to reason,
d) adherence to the magisterium,
e) holiness – humility, freedom and joy, and
f) seeking the edification of the Church.[38]

## Call to re-conversion towards a synodal Church

This is the deep cultural tradition into which Pope Francis is leading when he speaks of the path of synodality along which God is calling us. The Pope is not only speaking to a culture built around shared values, beliefs and assumptions about the mission, values and purpose of the organisation (in this case the Church as referred to in Chapter 3) but he is also challenging the institution to be consistent with its mission, values and beliefs.

While the 'Synod of Bishops' refers to the formal structure of collegiality between bishops and pope, the word 'synod' literally means travelling together. Francis makes it clear that his vision of synodality embraces journeying together – laity, pastors, the Bishop of Rome – an easy concept to put into words, but not so easy to put into practice.[39] More than a way of discerning, such 'journeying together' is at the heart of 'being Church'. It is inseparable from the pilgrim Church following Jesus the Way as fellow-travellers discerning the Kingdom of God in each period of history; it characterises both the life and the mission of the young and old, men and women of every culture and horizon who comprise the People of God. Synodality shapes 'the Body of Christ, in which we are members one of another, beginning with those who are pushed to the margins and trampled upon'.[40]

Synodality is, thus, inseparable from the communion of all those who are united by Baptism. In the Eucharist, those followers come together as *ecclesia* in the name of 'the Father, Son and holy Spirit'. They begin their assembly by seeking reconciliation with each other and with God; they listen to the Word and reflect upon it in their lives; they share the same bread and wine; and finally they go out on mission to evangelise in their world. There are formal structures at different levels in the Church for the expression of synodality, but in a synodal Church, they are 'only the most evident manifestation of a dynamism of communion which inspires all ecclesial decisions'.[41]

In summary, a synodal Church is the People of God, prayerful and humble as they reflect in community, open to – and guided by – the Holy Spirit to discern their mission in this time and history. It is a re-discovery of discipleship and community. It includes mutuality and a sense of partnership and respect for all the faithful. However, evangelisation is always the essential mission of the Church. So synodality is always synodality for mission.[42] 'The proclamation of Jesus Christ, dead and risen, who has revealed the Father and imparted the Spirit, is the fundamental vocation of the Christian community.'[43] In the words of Ormond Rush, 'a synodal Church is a Church that listens to the Spirit communicating through the sense of all the faithful, the *sensus fidelium*'.[44]

If the discernment about circumcision in Jerusalem exemplified synodality in the beginnings of the Church's life, then the 2019 Amazonian Synod could be seen as an anticipation of the synodal Church Francis speaks to. The process for the Amazon Synod and its Final Document centred on dialogue and conversion. The question before the Synod was: how might the Church be with the peoples of the Amazon? Austen Ivereigh remarks that:

> ... to answer that question the synod had to ask what kind of Church it would be if it heard the cry of the poor and the cry of the earth 'as one cry' and responded as Christ would. The way toward an answer was in the final document: a Church that is permanently undergoing a fourfold conversion – cultural, pastoral, ecological, and synodal...

That is, a synodal Church is a Church which is, at once, missionary and merciful in its pastoral outreach, culturally engaged with peoples, ecologically attuned and open and listening, especially to the poor and neediest.[45]

## Synodality and subsidiarity

One cluster of characteristics to be highlighted here relates to participative, empowering and grassroots leadership. These all are pertinent to the concept of synodality which has been part of Pope Francis' language as well as part of the briefs relating to the Plenary Council agenda in the Australian Church. The Pope's call for synodality has provoked debate, maybe because for Francis, synodality is not just about governance but about 'a way of being Church'[46]. Perhaps we could see Francis' synodality as an elaboration of Benedict XVI's 'co-responsibility'. In Pope Francis' own words,

> ... the Pope is not, by himself, above the Church; but within it as one of the baptised, and within the College of Bishops as a Bishop among Bishops, called at the same time – as Successor of Peter – to lead the Church of Rome which presides in charity over all the Churches.[47]

Another pertinent concept that has a long tradition in the Catholic Church is that of 'subsidiarity', which appeared in Pope Leo XXIII's encyclical *Rerum Novarum* in 1891 on its fortieth anniversary in *Quadragesimo Anno* of Pope Pius XI. (This will be discussed in more detail in Chapter 5.) Both 'synodality' and 'subsidiarity' have a long history in the Church and significant implications for leadership and culture in faith communities.

It might seem obvious to state that the challenge to the Church of our time is not the challenge of the Australian Church in any other time, place or culture. Yet, how consciously have some of the current structures and processes been adopted and maintained? It is a challenge and an ongoing work to hew out an understanding and language of cultural leadership which is shared by all those who work for the Church's mission and its various ministries.

## Synodality and collaboration in leadership

Collaboration in ministry is one way of expressing communion in ministry. It is just one element of the complex concept which is synodality. It might be useful to pause here to reflect briefly on this one element and how it is exercised in our ministries.

As cultural leaders, we suggest it might be useful to ask from time to time how policies and practices of a given ministry or agency (diocese, parish, education office, health system, PJP,) support and encourage effective relationships and pastoral teamwork in different areas of ministry? What are the indicators that we are ministering 'in community', that we are promoting collaboration and relationships?

To follow our messages about mission alignment and a culture built on relationships, we would suggest we don't all have to do everything and be in competition with each other. Whatever the area of ministry, we are one Church. Taking another example from education: schools in one diocese build on their strengths by sharing resources and ideas; each grows stronger, because of the quality of an initiative, maybe because they are emboldened by sensing they are part of a larger whole. On the other hand, in another diocese, schools vigorously and diligently row their boats in isolation: not drawing on solutions that a neighbouring school might have; not sharing their solutions; inadvertently and unintentionally developing a sense of competition that erodes a sense of well-being and shared mission. The authors have witnessed a Catholic high school leader in a remote island setting reach out a hand to his colleagues in the local government and Wesleyan schools to work together on improving curriculum options for the students in their respective schools. The relationships are authentic. That feels and smells like synodality to us. We assume such increased collaboration is occurring in Catholic health, social service and pastoral ministries.

In a similar fashion, the collaboration between parishes and ministries is critical for a sharing culture of wisdom and experience, even more so because lay pastoral ministries in Australia are still in the first generation or so. Such networking enhances the potential for groups of parishes to build on each other's strengths and experiences, through an exchange of ideas, resources, and most importantly, people, in shared ongoing learning, mentoring and even joint projects.

## Conclusion

Those who wish to be leaders in a synodal Church are signing up to work with others in a distinctive way. For Pope Francis, a synodal Church is characterised by the valuing of each person's charism, a dynamic of relationship and co-responsibility, through conversion of the heart and readiness for mutual listening. A synodal Church seeks to become a participatory and co-responsible Church in which no-one is put aside, and in which the contributions of all lay faithful – young, female and male, consecrated persons, groups, associations and movements – are welcomed.

The Final Document resulting from the Amazon Synod expressed in the words of the Amazonian Church this understanding of the Church moving towards the future:

> In order to walk together, the Church today needs a conversion to the synodal experience. It needs to strengthen a culture of dialogue, reciprocal listening, spiritual discernment, consensus and communion in order to find areas and ways of joint decision-making and to respond to pastoral challenges. In this way, co-responsibility in the life of the Church will be fostered in a spirit of service ... Synodality is a constitutive dimension of the Church. We cannot be Church without recognising a real practice of the *sensus fidei* of all the People of God.[48]

This is the understanding of 'synodal Church' to which we are attempting to respond in the following pages. The implications of that vision for leadership within the Church, while being signalled, are less developed. We believe that the theory and practice of leadership in the secular domain can illuminate the journey towards synodality for the Church. The next chapter considers perspectives on cultural leadership from contemporary theory and good practice.

## Activity 4.1: Reflection on the early Church's discernment

You might do this individually and/or in a small group. Put yourself into a space conducive to reflection. Become mindful of quietening yourself. Take a few moments to acknowledge the presence of God in your life and in the passage you are about to read.

Read Acts 15:1-36.

Re-read the passage slowly. Now, pause and put yourself in the position of one of those women and men in the story. Perhaps you are one of the advocates on behalf of the Gentile Churches; perhaps you represent the Church in Jerusalem. Try and be present to the story as it unfolds as you re-read (or listen to) the account in Acts once more.

- How do you feel as the reading unfolds?
- How might you have been changed had you been one of the players at the time?
- What words/phrases surprise you in this reading?
- Choose words/phrases that you will take away from this reading?

## Activity 4.2: Building collaborative communities

In the chapter above, we suggested that it might be useful to reflect on how policies and practices of a given ministry or agency support and encourage effective relationships and pastoral teamwork in and between different areas of ministry? From your own perspective:

What would you expect to see?

- In what ways does your agency promote collaboration between your agency and others?

## Endnotes

1. Pope Paul VI, Apostolic Letter, *Apostolica Sollicitudo* (hereafter AS), Establishing the Synod of Bishops for the Universal Church, Libreria Editrice Vaticana, 15th September 1965.
2. For example, *The Ministerial Priesthood and Justice in the World* in 1971, *On Catechesis for Our Time* in 1977, *The Vocation and Mission of the Family in the Church in the Contemporary World*, 2015.
3. For example, Oceania Synod in 1998 and the Pan-Amazonia Synod in 2019.
4. Cardinal Donald Wuerl, On Collegiality and Synodality, paper given at the annual convention of the Canon Law Society of America, 2016, https://www.ewtn.com/catholicism/library/on-collegiality-and-synodality-1257
5. Pope Francis, Address on the 50th Anniversary of the Institution of the Synod of Bishops, September 2015.
6. Pope Francis 2015.
7. Vatican II Council, *Christus Dominus*, (hereafter CD), in A. Flannery, Decree on the Pastoral Office of Bishops in the Church, #37.
8. International Theological Commission (hereafter ITC 2018). Synodality in the Life and Mission of the Church, 2018, #65. http://www.vatican.va/roman_curia/congregations/cfaith/cti_documents/rc_cti_20180302_sinodalita_en.html#
9. Pope Francis, General Audience, 23 October 2019.
10. *Final Document of the Synod of Bishops on Young People, Faith and Vocational Discernment*, (hereafter Synod on Youth) 2018, #122.
11. Pope Francis, 2015.
12. Acts 2:42-46.
13. Joseph Lam, Friendship and synodality: An ecclesiological suggestion on the eve of the Australian plenary council 2020, *The Australasian Catholic Record*, 97:2, 2020, pp.156-171.
14. Acts 2:2-3.
15. Acts 20:22-24.
16. Acts 6:1-6.
17. Acts 15:1-35; Rudolph Schnackenburg, Community co-operation in the New Testament, 1972, in G. Mannion, R. Gaillardetz, J. Kerkhofs & K. Wilson (eds), *Readings in Church Authority, Gifts and Challenges for Contemporary Catholicism*, Ashgate Publishing, Aldershot, 2003, pp. 152-154. ITC 2018 gives a detailed account of the Council of Jerusalem process, #19-22.
18. Acts 15:22, 28.
19. ITC 2018, #22.
20. ITC Sensus Fidei in the Life of the Church, 2014, #122.
21. Jan Kerkhofs, Synodality and Collegiality – the Dynamics of Authority, in Mannion et al, p. 149.
22. Schnackenburg, p.154.
23. Cardinal Leon-Jozef Suenens, Co-responsibility in the Church, 1968, in Mannion et al, p. 175.
24. Vatican II, *Constitution on Divine Revelation, Dei Verbum*.
25. Myriam Wijlens, Primacy-Collegiality-Synodality. Refiguring the Church because of *sensus fidei*, reprint from Peter Szabo, ed, Primacy and Synodality: Deepening Insights, Proceedings of the 23rd Congress of the Society for the Law of the Eastern Churches, September 3-8, 2017.
26. A major source for this section is ITC 2014.
27. LG, #12.
28. Ormond Rush, Plenary Council Participation and Reception: Synodality and Discerning the Sensus Fidelium,, Theological Studies 78:2, 2017, pp. 295-325.
29. Yves Congar op, 1981, in Mannion et al, p. 315.
30. ITC 2014 #60.
31. LG #12.
32. Myriam Wijlens, Reforming the Church by Hitting the Reset Button: Reconfiguring Collegiality within Synodality because of sensus fidei fidelium, The Canonist 8, 2017, reprinted for IAG Symposium, Sydney 4 March 2020, pp. 11-13.
33. Pope Francis Interview with Spadaro, 2013, Libreria Editrice Vaticana, #49-50, http://www.vatican.va/content/francesco/en/speeches/2013/september/documents/papa-francesco_20130921_intervista-spadaro.html
34. ITC 2014, #74.
35. ITC 2014, #49.
36. ITC 2014, #72-73.
37. ITC 2014, #118.
38. ITC 2014, #88-113.
39. Pope Francis, 2015.
40. Synod on Youth, #121.
41. Pope Francis, 2015.
42. Pope Francis, Letter to the Pilgrim People of God in Germany, 29 June 2019, #6 (quoting Pope Paul VI, *Evangelii Nuntiandi*, #14.)
43. Synod on Youth, #133.
44. Ormond Rush, p. 302.
45. Pope Francis, Apostolic Exhortation Querida Amazon, 2 February 2020; Final Document, The Amazon: New Paths for the Church and for an Integral Ecology, October 2019; Austen Ivereigh, Exposing the Spirit, What the Amazon Synod decided and what it revealed. Commonweal, 1 November 2019, https://www.commonwealmagazine.org/exposing-spirits
46. Massimo Faggioli, Pope Francis' struggle to bring forth a synodal Church, *La Croix International*, 26 December 2018.
47. Pope Francis, 2015.
48. Final Document, Amazonian Synod, #88.

# Chapter 5

# Cultural, Transrelational and Synodal Leadership

In an address to a group of Catholic leaders in 2015, Bishop Eamon Martin expressed reservations about defining leadership for his audience because a Google search he undertook turned up 492 million results for the word 'leadership' and 106 million for Catholic leadership. A similar Amazon search identified 20,000 books on the subject.[1] It seems as though everything has probably been said about this construct. It is therefore with self-conscious enthusiasm that we attempt to incorporate the weighty tome of contemporary theory of 'leadership' into something understandable and useful to lay leaders and ministers.

To accomplish this, we will bring together the perspectives we have acquired through many years of writing, research, practice and teaching in the area of leadership and consider what this may mean for church leaders pursuing a model of synodality. In this way we hope to help leaders discover for themselves the place of this form of cultural and relational leadership in their personal, professional and community lives. In Chapter 3 we introduced the reader to the concept of culture and how it is influenced by leadership, while in Chapter 4 we looked at what a synodal culture would look like in the Church and how leadership may be experienced in such a culture. Here we will offer insights into how this view of leadership has evolved.

## Definitions

A starting point for understanding leadership as relational and synodal might be to ask, 'what do people expect of people who have influence over them in some sphere of their lives?' Cameron's reflection on this is that we expect them:

> '... to act morally whereby they will not produce harm but rather will show the virtues of doing good, of honouring others, of taking positive stands, and of behaving in ways that clearly show that their own self-interests are not the driving motivation behind their leadership...'[2]

His reflection is helpful both in response to this question and in expanding upon the definition of 'leadership' (that we used in the Introduction) where we referred to leadership as being 'an influencing relationship'.

This aspect of leadership captures the major shift that has occurred in the way leadership has been viewed over the past century: from a perception of leadership as a science of management and administration preoccupied with the actions of the leader founded on a perception of people as objects of production, to the current position of a more subjective values-based exercise of influence for meaning, ownership and morality within relationships. In this latter view, leadership is achieved through the creation of quality relationships with everyone in the process through the understanding that the leader's own self-interests are not the driving motivation behind these relationships. Rather, it must be the moral good of all involved that is the motivator. We see this *serving of others'* interests view of leadership as incorporating ethical, moral, visionary and transrelational foundations.

The great Canadian philosopher Christopher Hodgkinson, putting it simply, described this approach by stating that what changes in leadership is context; what does not change is human nature. Human nature and relationships just happen to be the essential raw material of administration and leadership.[3]

Hodgkinson was telling us that it is not the thousands of characteristics and traits of leaders that authors have identified and written about for ages that matter, but the character of the person leading and how their character is recognised and responded to by others. The importance of character and relationships also suggests the importance of trust above all else in these relationships. The difficulty with the fundamental importance of trust in relationships is that it runs counter to the concept of control, something that can be attested to by anyone living in partnership with another.

Early theories of leadership focused on control for individual and organisational purposes. While this could be productive in the short term, the 'other' in such a relationship eventually became convinced that the whole purpose of the exercise was to meet the leader's needs and not theirs and as a result disengaged from the relationship. The

Martin Luther King Jr

legitimate pursuit of the goals of the organisation may have created a formal justification for this self-interest, but if the impact on the other remained unappreciated and trust was not achieved, the relationship and its goals usually failed. Much has changed in society over time, yet some organisations still hold, or have been forced to keep, old visions and practices of leadership. Be it for reasons of power, profit or tradition, we still see organisations today focusing on the power of the leader and not the integrity and quality of the relationships that are experienced because of that leadership (a condition within some leadership in the Church, as identified in earlier chapters).

## Values

In a Church that values synodality, these issues of character, relationships, moral purpose and trust appear even more important than when experienced in secular society. A pursuit of leadership that reflects these characteristics of a synodal Church still seems to remain elusive. The challenge for this chapter is to set the scene for what cultural leadership for a synodal Church may involve.

The study of leadership over the ages suggests that historically it has been surrounded by uncertainty. This uncertainty may derive from the complexity of leadership itself because of the competing and complementary domains in which it is practised and experienced. The figure below expresses these competing and complementary domains.

## The Leadership Domains

The values and beliefs that give direction to the faith and understandings of life for the leader contribute to the differing philosophies and theologies that give structure and meaning to their actions. At the same time, the morality and ethics of our leadership are immersed in relationships with the people involved in the exercise, thereby introducing the complexities of human nature, and differing individual and group motivations and personalities. To further complicate the process, there is the need to address the purpose of the organisation that is being led. (This purpose can be as diverse, for example, as the joint celebration of a faith, the balancing of an institution's accounts, or the academic performance of students or the health of patients.) Believing, relating and managing are interesting bedfellows and can create a natural tension that leaders would easily recognise in their daily lives.

## From science to subjectivity

In the early part of the century, thoughts about leadership were dominated by an individualistic/scientific/linear/rational approach such as that developed by Fredrick Taylor and others who tried to develop a science of management based on time-and-motion studies.[4] Later in the 1940s and 1950s, Herbert Simon and others shifted the focus to being one of researching the behaviours of managers in pursuit of a picture of 'good management' – a movement referred to as the Trait theory or the 'great man' theory.[5] Given the cultural orientation of the times, leadership was assumed to be the prerogative of the male of the species; there was no room for 'pesky suffragettes or feminists' as leadership existed in strong individuals who were, it was assumed, almost always men.

In the 1950s and 1960s, the focus on leadership shifted to explaining leader behaviour in terms of the interplay of the demands of the role with the leader's personal and psychological needs. Approaches using this explanation were titled 'system theories'. The most popular of these were the works of Talcott Parsons, and Getzels and Guba.[6] These system theories were the precursors to the contingency or situational theories that directed leaders to analyse the maturity and motivation of their followers, the followers' capacities to carry out tasks, and how that matched with certain suggested styles of leadership. These styles ranged from 'direct command' by the leader with followers who had low job maturity, through coaching of followers with motivation but 'low skills', supporting followers with 'high skills' but low motivation, to a delegation style of leadership for followers who were high on job maturity and motivation as shown in the diagram below.[7]

Later the field shifted from 'style' of leadership with its emphasis on power resting in the leader, not the follower, to a search for 'excellence' in organisations. Here success was usually measured in economic terms and by what interaction of traits, behaviours, situations and group facilitation helped people to lead others to excellence. This emphasis led to an emerging sense that leadership was a more subtle influence expressed in relationships built around exchanges about purpose, and measured through achievement of these purposes and satisfaction with the relationships. Peter Vaill drew attention to this concept and described it as 'purposing' or the continuous stream of actions by an organisation's formal leadership which had the effect of inducing clarity, consensus and commitment regarding the organisation's basic purpose.[8] This shift led to an understanding that, contrary

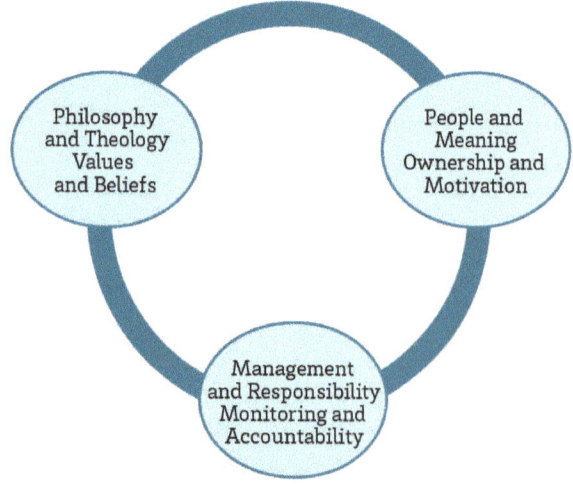

Figure 5.1. Domains of leadership

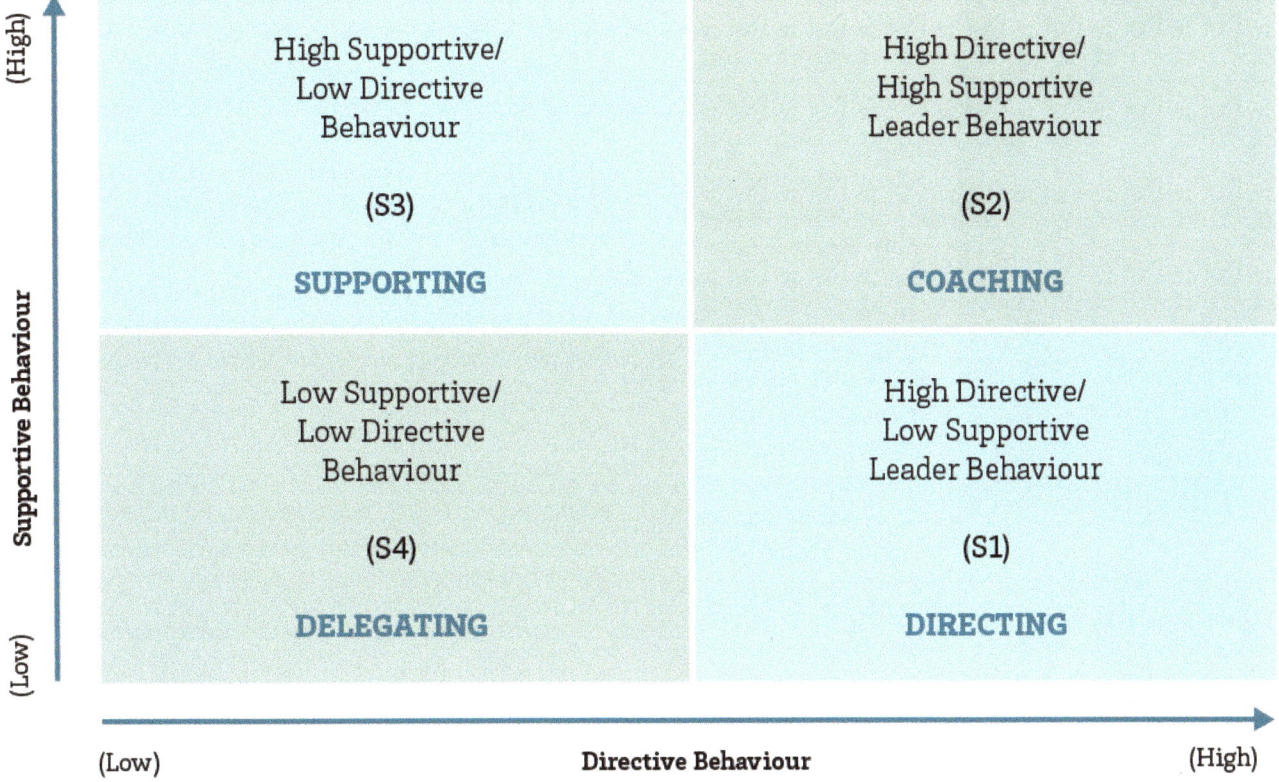

Figure 5.2. Hersey-Blanchard: Situational leadership theory (SLT).

to the thinking of the situational leadership approach, the leader's behavioural style is not as important as what the leader stands for and communicates to others. More important was the stirring of human consciousness, the enhancement of meaning about what the organisation is trying to achieve, and the spelling out of key cultural strands that provide both excitement and significance to work.

This emphasis towards meaning-making by leaders was also at the heart of one of the most important theoretical shifts in leadership approaches. This was captured in the research and writing of James MacGregor Burns, an historian and political scientist. Through his study of Franklin Delano Roosevelt, Mahatma Gandhi and others, MacGregor Burns shifted the focus of leadership to be as much on followers as on leaders. He saw leaders as inducing followers to act for certain goals that represent the values and the motivations, the wants and needs, the aspirations and expectations, of both leaders and followers.[9] He described two major components of such relationships related to purpose, these were described as 'transactional' and/or 'transforming' leadership.

Transactional leadership was seen as being driven by the exchange of valued 'things' between the leader and follower, things usually of a contractual nature. Transformational leadership occurred when one or more persons engaged in ways that raised one another to higher levels of motivation and moral behaviour, and consequently the leader and the follower were changed through this process at the moral level. He argued that leadership should be more than a leader doing deals (transactions) to get what he/she wants, but rather leaders should transform a group in ethically and morally significant ways. This led to the purposes and motivations of leaders and the other(s) in the relationship becoming fused, the moral level being raised, and leaders and followers both changing for the better. Shields argues that such a moral foundation gives this transformative approach to leadership the greatest potential for cultural change in the pursuit of hope and a better, more equitable future. She advocates for transformative leadership in a world characterised by volatility, uncertainty, complexity and ambiguity,[10] conditions we suggest are clearly evident in the Australian Catholic Church today.

## Values and purpose

The elements of transformational leadership resonate with the previously mentioned philosophy of Margaret Wheatley about leadership being 'how to support the workings of each other'[11] and the description of synodality and *sensus fidei* discussed previously. The period of 'transforming leadership' saw the field of leadership then shifting to focus on morality, values, vision and culture. In education, the work of Tom Sergiovanni and Jerry Starratt and others reflected this shift.[12] Sergiovanni introduced the idea of the 'forces of leadership' operating at five different levels: the technical, human, professional, cultural and the symbolic. The first three of these forces were seen as crucial to an effective organisation, with the last two linked to excellence. The important part of leadership was seen as resting in the cultural and symbolic level which gave meaning to the life of the

Jacinda Ardern

organisation through the modelling of moral actions by leaders' consistent emphases on core values.

Taking a similar approach, Starratt developed a model of cultural leadership using the illustration of the layers of an onion: the heart of the onion being the values and core beliefs of the culture as the essential elements of the missions which influenced the outer layers of the onion, which represented goals, programs and behaviours of the culture.[13] Starratt further suggested that leaders should understand that their role is to promote a vision that is driven by their own core values, and share this vision with others so that it is reflected and identified in the organisation or groups they lead.

Starratt's model starts with a core of values and beliefs that are basic to how the leader sees life. We view this emphasis as important to faith-based organisations such as Catholic parishes, schools and hospitals, as it emphasises how our core beliefs are the essential building block for how we lead. This concept was introduced in Chapter 1, especially in discussing the foundational belief of the disciple in the Christian faith. Without that foundational belief, the everyday actions of the leader will fail to bring the significance and meaning of the Jesus story into the lives of the individuals and groups being led.

Starratt used the onion model to generate an approach to cultural leadership that developed from a foundational belief about life. The steps show how this belief or value becomes the distinguishing feature of the leader, the culture of the institution and its people.

Starratt's model also espoused the principle of 'subsidiarity' which was referred to in reference to the Church's mission and culture from the terms origins in the Encyclical *Rerum Novarum* of Pope Leo XIII where it was described as

> ... that most weighty principle, which cannot be set aside or changed. Just as it is gravely wrong to take from individuals what they can accomplish by their own initiative and industry and give it to the community, so also it is an injustice and at the same time a grave evil and disturbance of right order

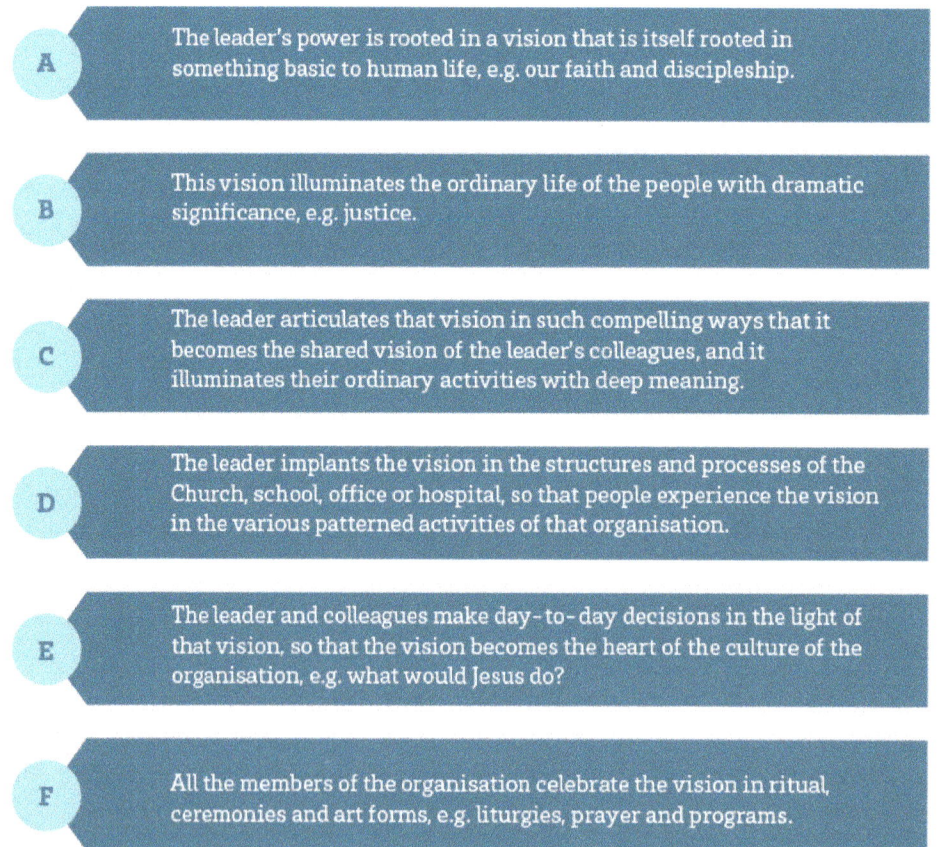

Figure 5.3. Starratt's vision for cultural leadership

to assign to a greater and higher association what lesser and subordinate organisations can do.[14]

In time, the Church applied the concept of subsidiarity to its own life, with Pope Pius XII concluding, 'These are surely enlightened words, valid for social life in all its grades and also for the life of the Church without prejudice to its hierarchical structure,'[15] Starratt saw this as fundamental to a mission of equity and justice, describing 'subsidiarity' from a secular perspective as the 'authority to make discretional decisions concerning work' and being placed 'as close to the work as possible ... [with the] persons closest to the task [being] given the authority and responsibility to carry out the task.'[16]

Other authors have followed a similar focus on leadership as being founded in the core values we hold and brought to life in our relationships with others. Peter Block saw leadership in terms of stewardship and our responsibility to serve others rather than ourselves.[17] Thomas Greenleaf described this service construct as being focused on the care taken by the servant to meet others' needs, especially those of least advantage. The best test, according to Greenleaf, is:

> ... do those served grow as persons; do they, while being served, become healthier, wiser, freer, more autonomous, more likely themselves to become servants? And what is the effect on the least privileged in society; will they benefit, or at least, not be further deprived?[18]

The characteristics of the Servant Leadership model highlight its links to transformational leadership and its congruency with the teachings and principles of most Christian Churches, including Catholicism. Greenleaf's servant leaders were seen as having the following characteristics: knowing their selves well, holding a liberating vision, having unlimited liability for others, using persuasion and influence, being community builders and using power ethically.

These characteristics are strongly embedded in Christian values and teachings about the life of Jesus Christ. They have become popular models for religious institutions as they emphasise the spiritual core of the leader as contrasted with the administrative and managerial elements of the process. The Greenleaf characteristics clearly incorporate many of the principles of transforming leadership with its emphasis on the morality of the process. While the shared characteristics of values-based approaches to leadership were in many cases equated with the life and leadership of Jesus Christ, attempts to support these characteristics from religious literature proved difficult. Even so, the comparison became part of the attraction of these theories to religious-based leadership programs and teachings. However, the success of these 'servant' approaches in Catholic education leadership and similar faith-based institutions proved problematic. Referencing the contemporary role of school principals, Branson points out that the many managerial and administrative demands and responsibilities upon them make it difficult for principals to 'achieve servant leadership on a regular basis'. An additional hurdle for principals of Catholic schools arises from the expectation that their servant leadership is based on that of Jesus Christ, and so 'many view it as God's theory and, thus, beyond their human capacity to achieve'.[19]

Despite this cautionary message, we will revisit these elements when discussing Branson and his associates' Transrelational Leadership model and its links to elements of the life of Jesus as leader through the witness captured in the Gospels.

The moral rightness of the action of leaders is foundational to these various approaches that have emerged from McGregor Burns' model of transformational leadership that focus on the service, morality and the ethics involved in the relationship.

## Moral and ethical leadership

Consistent with the insights of McGregor Burns, there was now a view of leading as a process requiring truth to one's values and beliefs.

Don Willower was an acknowledged leader in the field of educational leadership. In the 1980s and 1990s he argued that leadership should address the subjectivity of values and beliefs. In its way, this acknowledged the moral and ethical imperatives of the human condition. He proposed that experiences designed to help people lead should have two main characteristics: first, they should furnish broad visions of what human beings and institutions might become 'at their best'; secondly, they should speak realistically to the problem of concrete moral choice that is such a salient feature of leadership life.[20] In pursuing these goals of moral leadership, it is well to keep in mind that attempts to make wise moral choices may simply not work out much of the time as leaders attempt to navigate the complexities of modern organisations in times that are ethically ambiguous.[21]

This complexity often lies in the challenge for leaders to choose between two 'goods' rather than a 'good' and a 'bad'[22] In a postmodern world, an emphasis on objectivity and value neutrality creates the equally dangerous trap of relativism, whereby the validity of a 'good' simply rests in the personal preference of the individual. Seeking answers about the 'good' through the use of absolute truths or the relativism of personal preference are equally dangerous. Caroline Shields explained this danger of taking either position – the absolutist or the relativist – as it eliminates any need for dialogue or discernment.[23]

This moral leadership approach uses ethics as principles to help with this search for 'the good'. In this context ethics are generally viewed as the norms and virtues by which members of a community are bound to a way of living out their desirable and preferred values. Starratt suggests that ethics are maps that we consult only when the familiar terrain we are traversing becomes a tangle of underbrush. He names three particularly significant ethics. These are: (i) authenticity (calling for integrity in interactions), (ii) presence (calling for relationships that are open and engaging), and (iii) responsibility (recognising personal and corporate accountability). He uses the term 'virtues' to describe the living out of these three ethics, suggesting that he sees them clearly as a personally preferred priority of values that leaders can bring to their leadership role.[24] Another widely accepted ethical schema for leadership asked leaders to focus on their actions and decisions from the perspective of how the ethics of justice, care, critique, and the profession are preferred and actioned within the culture.[25]

Of course, while an appropriate moral philosophy can strengthen leadership, applications are always uncertain. There are no panaceas and no guarantees as the context in which leadership is exercised can vary immensely. What is usually at the heart of leadership is that it always occurs in relationships and that makes it complex. Later we will present a model and strategy utilising principles of discernment to help with the search for the elusive 'good'.

## Transrelational leadership

In their model of transrelational leadership, Branson and his associates extended the moral and ethical view of leadership with a new emphasis on complex relationships. They essentially viewed leadership as the capacity to build relationships through collegiality, cooperation and teamwork. In this way, no two leadership situations are the same, as the context of the relationships is unique and so must be the leader's approach. Incorporating many of the constructs discussed earlier, such leadership must create a culture of trust, openness, transparency, honesty, integrity, collegiality and ethical practice.[26] How can we best create such cultures with others? Branson and his colleagues suggested transrelational leadership is characterised by certain elements[27] which we have contrasted here in Figure 5.4 with the elements of transforming and transactional leadership discussed earlier.

Branson and his colleagues drew on previous researchers who proposed that prospective cultural leaders should develop the following elements:

1. be an in-group member
2. champion the group
3. shape the group's identity
4. align the group's identity to the wider reality.[29]

The essential demand of being an 'in-group member' is the call to know ourselves, know how we are 'best' in relationships, and know what the group members want from the outcomes of their relationships with us. While no one experience can best meet all the goals of developing self-awareness and awareness of others, tools such as the Johari Window, the Myers-Briggs type indicator, and others, can be helpful in regard to their focus on accurately recognising our own emotions, thoughts, and values and how they influence our behaviour. The importance of such exercises is to be able to accurately assess our strengths and limitations, especially when in relationships with others, so as to develop a well-grounded sense of confidence and optimism, with a growth mindset.[30] The development of such awareness is an important precursor to collegial dialogue and shared decision-making, giving the leader and others a better understanding of shared needs and the creation of opportunities to develop trust, understanding, collegiality, openness and transparency. Daniel Goleman's theories of

| Relational Dimensions of Leadership | | |
|---|---|---|
| Transactional Leadership | Transformational Leadership | Transrelational Leadership |
| Exclusive | Inclusive | Engaging |
| Top-down Control | Bottom-up Influence | Emerging Influence |
| Task-related Involvement | Meaningful Involvement | Purposeful Involvement |
| Outcomes Focused | People Focused | Future Focused |
| Inflexible | Flexible | Shared Expertise-Discovery |
| Roles/Responsibilities | Partnerships/Relational | Inter-relational/Networks |
| Leader as Expert | Shared Leadership | Interactive Leadership |
| Skill Learning | Organisational Learning | Holistic Learning |
| Attention to Performance | Attention to Capacity | Attention to Social Dynamics |
| High Accountability | Review/Reflect/Adapt | Imagination/Creativity |
| Success Goal-based | Celebrate Achievements | Risk Taking |
| | | Dialogical |

Figure 5.4. Contrasting leadership models [28]

emotional and social intelligence focus on the importance of self-actualisation, self-regulation, awareness of the needs of others, empathy towards their needs, and acceptable social skills. These theories give a strong foundation for an understanding of the necessary characteristics for the effective relational leader in secular cultures. These characteristics are, of course, also recognised as core to the establishment of relationships with members of a synodal Church.

The 'championing leader' characteristic captures the story of many of the leaders that James MacGregor Burns used to explain the difference between transactional and transforming leaders. Historical leaders such as Franklin Delano Roosevelt, Winston Churchill, Mother Teresa, Martin Luther King Jr, Golda Meir, Mahatma Gandhi and Nelson Mandela all showed they were 'of' the group and clearly understood the values, beliefs and behaviour of the people they were called on to lead. In practising their leadership, they modelled and proclaimed the important characteristics of their people and how they would confront challenges together. They stood as sources of support, affirmation and defence against external threats and internal doubts and fears, and communicated what was essential to survival in overcoming these challenges, be they prejudice, hatred, invasion or hopelessness.

These historical transforming leaders confronted challenges relating to periods of world war, Apartheid, the Great Depression, colonial occupation, racial discrimination and economic inequality. Current leaders face some of these challenges in addition to others related to climate change, the pandemic caused by the COVID-19 virus, the history of institutional child sexual abuse and a Church in a period of doubt and reform. A challenge shared by both past and contemporary leaders is to nurture the ability to affect the moral purpose and the sense of cohesion and meaning of the cultures they lead. The 'championing' of the group (or country) these transforming leaders represented lives on today in literature and history, well after their presence has passed.

In the same way, current leaders who touch peoples' lives and give meaning, purpose and fulfilment to membership of the group, especially during times of change and crises, will probably live on in the memories and stories of their people and places. Two examples of leadership in Australia that engendered wide-spread trust and commitment from the country early in 2020 were the examples of the New South Wales Chief Commissioner of the Bush Fire Brigade, and the Chief Medical Officer of Australia. Their regular media broadcasts during the devastating bushfires of Eastern Australia over the summer of 2020 and the COVID-19 pandemic of the same year were broadly seen as engendering deep levels of trust and assurance from the nation. They calmly gave expertise, direction and meaning to a period of danger and fear: they presented as humble and ordinary champions.[31]

'Shaping the group's identity' echoes Starratt's model discussed earlier, whereby the vision of the culture is articulated by the leader and shared with the group in such

Nelson Mandela

a compelling way that it becomes one part of the group's identity and purpose. We described this vision as being our sense of spirituality and faith. The shaping actions of the leader affirm and resource the efforts of members so that identified priorities become reinforced, celebrated and give form to the culture. The focus of conversations, staff meetings, celebrations, and renewal activities is to create organisational learning and growth. All these interactions can bring people together to be resources to each other, making connections happen with other sources, either internal or external. Resourcing and affirming the efforts of members that contribute to the goals of the culture becomes the prime focus of such a shaper-leader.

Similar to the shaping activities of the transrelational leader is the process of challenging members of the organisation to align the important issues they experience in their external context to their professional and personal activities. It includes bringing members into contact with literature, professional services and external sources that will progress and develop the activities of groups and individuals who have demonstrated internal commitment and ownership of renewal and development activities.

Interestingly, given our interest in a synodal culture of leadership in the Church, Branson and other transrelational leadership proponents have argued that Jesus demonstrated a leadership that exemplified these four characteristics of the

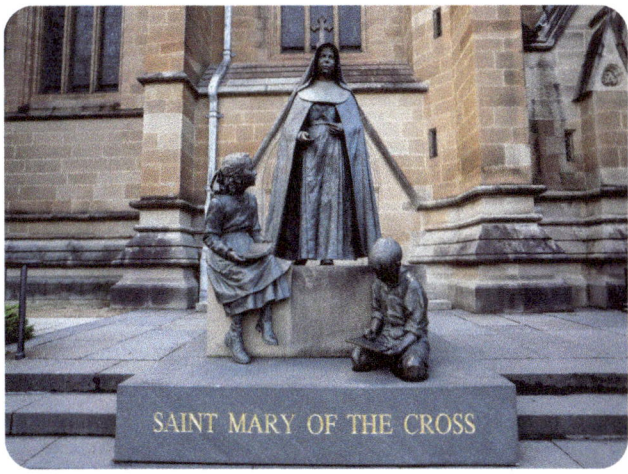

transrelational model of leadership. The comparison, as stated by Branson et al, can be summarised as follows:

- Jesus was 'in the group' of those who were the Jewish people of 1st century CE. He demonstrated consistently his sincere involvement in the suffering and expectations and general circumstances of the Jewish people, especially those who were poor and marginalised, but also those like the Pharisees with whom he engaged in debate. The key word in the model is 'sincere', reflecting a genuine relational capacity with the group.

- Jesus 'championed' the common Jewish people, as is demonstrated by his teaching about God's love for all. The Sermon on the Mount and the Beatitudes are given as examples of this championing, as well as Jesus sending out his disciples themselves to teach and heal in God's name.

- Jesus expanded the Jewish people's 'understanding of their identity' as God's chosen people, especially by challenging their view about the reign of God being only in the future. Further, his teaching about the Kingdom of God demonstrated that they, even those regarded as the greatest sinners, had a place in that Kingdom.

- Jesus engaged the Jewish people 'with their wider reality' by describing how God's Kingdom was not only for them but for all who seek it, including their enemies and those outside the Jewish religion. He challenged the Temple authorities against commercial action in the Temple precincts – God's sacred place.[32]

Using this lens, the leadership of Jesus can be viewed as transrelational and his teachings embedded in moral and values messaging. Elements of the transrelational leadership model being embedded in the moral and value challenges associated with relationships affected by the leader have been a consistent focus of writers and researchers on cultural leadership over the past thirty years.

## Conclusion

We have named just a few of the important contributors to our understanding of the transrelational approach to moral relational leadership. Most of the authors mentioned focused on the construct of 'moral purpose', with associated leadership processes variously described as 'moral literacy' (the ability to recognise, articulate and discern moral purpose); 'moral potency' (the strength and importance of the held moral position) and 'moral agency' (the capacity to action and live out a moral purpose).[33] Essentially, all these leadership foci view the ultimate effectiveness of the leadership process and the outcomes of cultural goals in a similar fashion. That is, as resting in the pursuit and fulfillment of the moral and ethical needs of all individuals affected by the leadership processes.

Building on this work, and reflecting on their practical experiences and research, Pettit and Burford raised questions about how we can best understand the processes that form value positions, and the forces that either help or hinder putting these value positions into action. They raised other questions. For example: How do the cultural contexts in which leaders operate impact on their values position? What are the processes that inform a leader's capacity for moral discernment in decision-making? Why are a person's values not necessarily translated into actions based on values?[34]

Chapter 8 will introduce a model designed by these authors to help answer these and other questions. Chapter 8 will give a foundation for moral discernment as an aid for development of transrelational leadership in a synodal Church.

## Activity 5.1: Effective leaders

You may care to reflect on your experiences of an effective leader and an ineffective leader, and critique these experiences against your understanding of cultural leadership as fundamentally being a relational phenomenon.

- What were the distinguishing leadership features of each of these leaders?
- Which of the past leadership theories would best describe this person's leadership style?
- In what ways did their relational capacity benefit or constrain their leadership practice?
- What is your considered opinion about the relative importance of relationships in the practice of cultural leadership?

## Activity 5.2: Transrelational leaders

Some reflections on leadership. Consider the example of three individuals who you consider are strong leaders that you admire. From the information you know about each of these, determine whether or not they displayed some or all of the four characteristics of leadership proposed in the transrelational model of leadership.

- Which of these four characteristics are leadership strengths?
- Ask a professional colleague to describe your approach to leadership and compare their feedback with your own impressions.

## Activity 5.3: Working at our best

Willower (1981) told us that a conception of values that would aid advancement in leadership should have two main characteristics: first it should furnish broad visions of what human beings and institutions might become at their best; second, it should speak realistically to the problem of concrete moral choice that is such a salient feature of leadership life.

- Selecting a matter of concern or tension within your team or staff, elect to take time at your next meeting to individually reflect on what the team/board/school/parish/department might look like if it were working 'at its best' in reaction to this challenge.
- Share your reflection with a team of three and then decide what important 'best' elements can be shared with the whole group.
- Add reflections about what the challenge of being 'at our best' might look like in this situation being discussed.

## Endnotes

1. Archbishop Eamon Martin, Opening address to Annual Round Table Discussion, Marino Institute of Education, March 2015.
2. Kim S. Cameron, *Competing Values Leadership: Creating Value in Organisation*, Edward Elgar Publishing, 2006, p. 187.
3. C. Hodgkinson, *Administrative philosophy: Values and motivations in administrative life*, Redwood Books, Trowbridge, UK, 1996.
4. Fredrick Taylor, *The Principles of Scientific Management*, Harper and Row, New York, 1911.
5. Herbert Simon, *Administrative Behaviour*, Macmillan, New York, 1950.
6. See Talcott Parsons, The Present Status of 'Structural-Functional' Theory in Sociology, *Social Systems and The Evolution of Action Theory*, The Free Press, New York, 1975, and W. Getzels & E. G. Guba, Social Behavior and the Administrative Process, *The School Review*, 65:4, Winter, 1957, pp. 423-441.
7. See P. Hersey & K. Blanchard, *Management of Organizational Behaviour: Utilizing Human Resources*, Prentice-Hall, Englewood Cliffs, 1982.
8. P. B.Vaill, Practice Theories in Organization Development, *Academy of management proceedings*, 1971, pp. 161-170.
9. J. M. Burns, *Leadership*, Harper & Row, New York, 1978.
10. C. M. Shields, *Transformative Leadership in Education*, Taylor and Francis Group, New York, 2017, p. 4.
11. M. Wheatley, 2006. p. 132.
12. For example, for those who wish to read more, see T. J. Sergiovanni & R. J. Starratt, *Supervision: A redefinition* (8th ed.), McGraw Hill, New York, 2007.
13. R. J. Starratt, *Cultivating an ethical school*, Routledge, New York, 2012.
14. Pope Leo XIII, Encyclical *Rerum Novarum*, 1891.
15. Quoted in Andrew Murray, The Principle of Subsidiarity and the Church, *Australasian Catholic Record* 72:2, 1995, pp. 163-175.
16. R. Starratt, *Transforming Educational Administration: Meaning, Community and Excellence*, Mc Graw-Hill, New York, 1996, p. 121.
17. See Peter Block, *Stewardship: Choosing Service Over Self-Interest*, 2nd Edition, Berrett-Koehler Publishers, 2013.
18. R. K. Greenleaf, 1970. 'The Servant as Leader,' sighted in Branson & Al, p..2.
19. Branson, 2019, p..2.
20. D. Willower, Educational administration: Some philosophical and other considerations, *Journal of Educational Administration*, 19:2, 1981, pp. 115-140. We have incorporated such reflective processes in Chapter 10 which will deal with the development of future leaders in the church.
21. See P. Duignan, *Educational Leadership: Key challenges and ethical challenges*, Cambridge University Press, 2007.
22. See P. Duignan & C. Burford, Preparing educational leaders for the paradoxes and dilemmas of contemporary schooling, paper presented at the British Educational Research Association Annual Conference, Exeter, 2003
23. C. Shields, Ethical Leadership: A Critical Transformative Approach in C. Branson and S. Gross (eds), *Handbook of Ethical Educational Leadership*, Routledge, New York, 2014, p. 28.
24. R. J. Starratt, *Cultivating an ethical school*, Routledge, New York, 2012.
25. J. P. Shapiro & J. A. Stefkovich, *Ethical leadership and decision making in education: Applying theoretical perspectives to complex dilemmas*, Erlbaum, Mahwah, 2001.
26. Branson et al, 2019, p. 4.
27. Ibid.
28. C. Burford & C. Branson, Leading Self, Leading Community, Unit EDLE681, Master of Educational Leadership, Australian Catholic University, 2015.
29. S. A. Haslam, S. D. Reicher & M. J. Platow, *The new psychology of leadership, Identity, influence and power*, Psychology Press, Hove and New York, 2013.
30. See Goleman, 2006.
31. Tony Wright, Brendan Murphy, the steady Doc who became a star, makes his exit, Opinion, *Sydney Morning Herald*, 26 June 2020.
32. Branson et al, 2019, p. 7.
33. See S. T. Hanna, & Avolio, B. J., Moral potency: Building the capacity for character-based leadership, *Consulting Psychology Journal: Practice and Research*. 62:4, 2010, pp. 291-310; A. Bandura, Selective moral disengagement in the exercise of moral agency, Journal of Moral Education, 31:2, 2002, pp.101-119; M. Bezzina & N. Tuana, From awareness to action: some thoughts on engaging moral purpose in educational leadership' (unpublished manuscript, limited circulation), 2012.
34. C. Burford, C. & P. Pettit, A Conceptual Model for Linking Values, Discernment and outcome Perception, *Values and Ethics in Educational Administration*, 13:2, March 2018, pp. 1-9.

# Chapter 6

# Governance Serving Mission in a Synodal Church

Having begun with mission as the definer of the Church's identity and purpose and the starting point for leadership, we explored culture and the role of leaders in shaping mission-effective cultures, especially as they relate to a synodal Church. In this chapter, we focus on the interface between leadership, culture and issues related to governance as they pertain to a synodal Church.

## Good governance builds cultures to drive mission

It is axiomatic that the work of governance is one of the critical functions of leaders in any organisation. It is not the core mission of the organisation, nor its primary work. Good governance is at the service of the mission and at the service of those who are engaged in a particular ministry. Governance involves processes of moral discernment that can be either assisted or impeded by the structures by which it operates. Not all governance is effective or appropriate. Not all governance is consistent with the mission and synodal culture of the Church. And the reality is that governance, administration, people, culture and their environments are all inextricably entwined in any organisation, including in ministries of the Church.

Our understanding of 'governance' is inclusive of the processes that: drive an organisation's direction; build its culture and resources to achieve its goals; regulate its legal compliance; monitor, improve and report on its performance; and communicate with stakeholders. The role of governance therefore includes setting its vision and strategic priorities, establishing high-level structures to achieve its mission, approving resourcing (at a high level), monitoring performance against goals and ethical standards, being accountable to stakeholders, monitoring and improving all these processes, being compliant with civil requirements and, in a Church context, attending to the requirements of Canon Law. Added to this broad list of functions are those named in the *LSC* report as

the system of rules, relationship and practices by which authority and control are exercised within organisations ... It encompasses the systems, structure and policies that control the way in which any institution operates, and the mechanisms by which the institution, and its people, can be held to account.[1]

Good governance is essential in ensuring that an organisation will achieve what it was created to achieve (whether, for example, that is to create profit, or environmental housing or a combination of both), and to do so ethically and ensure its future viability while reporting fully and openly to its stakeholders. Put another way, good governance will 'drive good cultures, support good leadership and build trust in the institution'[2]. For leaders in the Church, responsibility within their governance function is to discern how governance can best serve the mission of the Church.

Structures for governance vary and can involve a range of governing bodies such as Boards, Trustees and Councils. Particular mechanisms for dioceses, parishes and religious institutes are outlined in the Revised Canon Law of 1983.[3] In the case of schools sponsored by religious institutes, the governance structure usually involves an incorporated College Board, in most cases overseen by some kind of governing education Council legally established by a Religious Institute, with variances when schools are co-sponsored (for example, with a diocese). Schools coming under a Ministerial PJP (e.g. the schools that are part of Mary Aikenhead Ministries) are overseen by the governance structures within that PJP. The establishment of Ministerial PJPs, being relatively recent, has been very deliberate with a high level of attention given to their mandates, their delegations, relationships and governance structures. Most diocesan school systems and social service agencies are governed by some form of council, many of which are advisory only to the Bishop and are not legally incorporated. Some dioceses are moving towards incorporation of the school system. There is often less clarity about the scope and limitations of delegations in diocesan arrangements than in those of Ministerial PJPs.

## One mission: a variety of ministries, a plethora of tensions

The specifics of a call to mission vary from ministry to ministry, whether it is as teacher or principal, academic or Trustee, health or welfare professional, parish and diocesan ministries, ordained or commissioned. Whatever the particular ministry, all leaders are confronted with the constant need to discern the fidelity of their organisation to its core mission. When leaders ask themselves 'what should I do in a given situation?' the implied reference point is the core mission of that ministry and the larger mission it serves. How can my leadership better serve the mission to make God present and visible in our world? How can I in my role better promote our mission to witness to a God of mercy and truth? How can I honour the values of our institute's charism?

Within each area of ministerial outreach, there is a further ethic arising from each of the professions pertinent to that area. For example, a Principal and Religious Education Coordinator need to weigh their discernment against the professional standards imposed upon them as teachers, educators and curriculum specialists; managers in different departments in a healthcare system likewise must consider the requirements upon medical professionals, researchers and relevant sciences, and use these considerations to serve the mission better; the same can be said for social workers, counsellors and accountants and others who serve in administration; while those on Boards, Councils and Diocesan and Parish Finance committees need to strengthen the exercise of their particular professional ethic by drawing on best practice in governance.

Within the context of their overall mission, leaders are constantly involved in decision-making which more often than not requires moral discernment; they are responsible for governance that promotes a culture that is faithful to the values and beliefs of the larger mission which, at the same time, honours the values and principles of the profession (or professions) specific to a given ministry and its organisational context.

Balancing these different value-sets and principles can be complex, compromising and lead to dissonance across the various communities with which a particular ministry engages. This is the reality of leadership and the moral discernment it demands: it is mostly multifaceted and messy. It would be unhelpful to downplay the complexity of determining the best way forward. Legislation in various countries around Voluntary-Assisted Dying (VAD) and Abortion and Marriage Equality illustrate this as obvious examples. Similarly, there was contention when schools re-opened for face-to-face teaching during the COVID-19 crisis, or when and by how much to increase staff salaries in the middle of the Covid-19 recession. Those who expect that their governance decision-making will be in simple black-and-white terms will probably make some poor decisions. Experienced leaders know well that decision-making is seldom a choice between a clear-cut 'good' and 'bad', and more frequently a choice between 'good' and 'better' or between 'bad' and 'not so bad'.

Our purpose in this book is to offer from our experience suggestions for ways to facilitate greater fidelity to mission while negotiating some of these tensions.

## Starting point: 'good' governance

In descriptions of 'good' governance, there is a pattern of recurring words, including: 'integrity', 'accountability', 'responsibility' or 'stewardship', 'transparency' or 'openness'. In the secular sphere of companies and commerce, good governance is generally understood to presume processes that are participatory and collaborative, inclusive, transparent, future-oriented, and committed to improvement.[4] These are seen as essential if governance, in Robert Fitzgerald's words, is to 'promote integrity, legitimacy and the just exercise of authority'[5].

What kind of governance is consistent with a Church that is synodal in character? In the first instance, governance in the Church and its ministries should meet the basic requirements of good governance in the secular sphere. We recall Pope Francis' vision for a synodal Church. There is much in the secular understanding of good governance that is in harmony with this vision of Pope Francis'.

However, corporate good governance has limits in terms of synodality. In advance of the German Synod in 2020, Pope Francis wrote to the Bishops and all the People of God in Germany, warning them that to give in to the temptation to believe that solutions to the Church's current and future problems would 'come only from purely structural or bureaucratic reforms' would run the risk of not touching the 'vital nuclei that need attention'.[6]

In other words, as a Church, the Pope warned, we would be mistaken to attempt to 'fix' our Church and its culture simply through changing structures or by bringing a corporate-sector approach to leadership and governance. We might feel more secure against legal challenges and financial scandals, but such an approach, in itself, is insufficient. The Pope continues in his letter:

> At the heart of this temptation there is the thought that, faced with so many problems and shortcomings, the best response would be to reorganise things, make changes and indulge in 'mending' in order to adapt the life of the Church to the prevailing logic or the logic of a particular group.[7]

Following this path, he warned, it could seem that everything will be resolved if only we could do away with the tensions of our human existence and, he added, those tensions 'that the Gospel itself wants to create'. While it is important to pay attention to these things and reflect on them, he wrote, they in themselves are not our faith. Our mission and raison d'être consist in the mystery of God revealed in Jesus. 'Without a new life and an authentic evangelical spirit, without the Church's fidelity to her vocation, any new structure is corrupted in a short time.'

He reminded the German Church that their meeting, unique as it was, with an equal number of clerical and lay participants, was in essence, a *synodos* 'under the guidance of the Holy Spirit'[8]. In beautiful phrases, he urged them 'to be invaded by the Spirit, to learn to listen and discern the ever-new horizon that is always on offer. Synodality presupposes and requires the irruption of the Holy Spirit' . It is a message full of hope for the potential – and the challenge – of the 'ever-new horizon' that is there for our discerning.

## Governance processes for a synodal Church

In the words of the LSC report,

> Within the Church, good governance will rest on clear structures and accountabilities, a commitment to ecclesial and civil governance principles, a supporting ethical culture, effective communication, right relationships, consequences for wrong actions and good leadership …

Echoing some of our earlier discussion, the LSC report concluded that good governance 'is as much about character as capability, about discernment as judgement, about integrity as compliance, and about ethics and values as processes and protocols'[9].

Building on the accepted norms for good governance in the civil sphere, we can reflect again on our understanding of 'synodality'. As summarised previously, a synodal Church is one displaying these characteristics: an attitude of conversion; a culture of inclusion, dialogue and mutual listening; an openness to discern the Spirit; processes of joint decision-making which seek consensus in a way which strengthens the community of the faithful; and always a spirit of service to pastoral challenges and the mission begun by Jesus Christ.[10] These characteristics are not discrete. They work cohesively. We will discuss each of these hallmarks of a synodal Church very briefly and hint at implications for governance.

### (i) A synodal Church is mission-oriented in its response to pastoral challenges

We have discussed mission in previous chapters. Mission-oriented implies a spirit of service that has been a precious legacy in our Church over the centuries in the lives of individuals and groups, as exemplified by religious institutes.

While most of those in ministerial governance are familiar with keeping a mission focus central as they balance the discernment of priorities (from among many compelling demands on their attention), a synodal Church which is mission-oriented cannot rest on its past achievements. Pope Francis keeps challenging us as the People of God to be ever more pastorally creative and proactive in mission, to stay alert to the pastoral challenges of our times and to be there, 'on the edge'. In 2015, for example, he challenged Catholic educators, to be masters of reasonable risk, among other things, and to go to the peripheries[11], just as he previously challenged priests to be shepherds who, in their closeness to people, live with 'the smell of the sheep'[12].

This is a particular challenge for Catholic education which began as a radical outreach to those in greatest need. Over centuries of diligent professionalism, Catholic schools have become more and more successful, but often less accessible by those in greatest need. Some Catholic schools (and systems) have worked hard to counter this. Yet it has been apparent for some years that the poorest children, even the poorest Catholic children, are not in Catholic schools.[13] This hardly aligns with a Church 'oriented especially towards the poor, the marginalised and those on the edge'[14]. With the best of intentions, leaders in education struggle with this tension, as do their colleagues in health with a parallel challenge. Leaders who have attempted to address this tension of mission and pastoral challenge have had to deal with this through multiple layers of moral discernment.

Earlier we named a few of the issues of our times.[15] Governance in a synodal Church seeks to discern what actions or initiative or practice in an organisation should be a priority in support of the mission at this point in time. The Church is called to bring an incarnational dimension to discernment of priorities and areas of mission. In a complex world, where is the revelation of God's love most needed now? It is inspiring to observe many religious institutes, having entrusted their apostolates of education and health to lay leaders, now seeking out these new peripheries of mission.

This raises questions about how priorities are determined, by whom, and against what principles. It is important to identify the reasons for naming a strategic direction at a given time. Likewise, it is important to identify the reasons for excluding other directions. Why are we choosing this direction now? Why are we not choosing this alternate direction?

Building a mission culture requires information, facts and evidence, a passion for showing the face of a merciful God in our world, and imagination for what might be possible. How do those in governance in an agency or institution identify the areas of pastoral need and challenge at any one point in time? The six broad statements summarising the mission of a post-Vatican II Church identified earlier also suggest some starting questions: How does a Board (or Leadership Team) know if the strategic direction, policies, budget priorities and communications of their agencies reflect a community inspired by the Word? How can they be sure they are oriented towards the poor and marginal? How do they facilitate effectiveness in their mission? How do they demonstrate an integrated ecological consciousness?

Another way of considering this set of mission-oriented questions is to ask the following: How is how our health ministry different because of our mission? In what way are our schools and universities different because they are driven by Jesus' mission? How are our welfare agencies different in scope, style and reach because of our mission? How is this suburb different because of the presence of the parish of St 'So-n-So?' How are the culture and communications of this diocesan office shaped by our mission?[16] For some, the answer might be as simple as: because we are here, because we are offering this service where it is most needed now.

### (ii) Synodal leaders develop a culture of inclusion, dialogue and mutual listening.

A culture of dialogue and mutual listening in an organisation fosters a culture of freedom and creativity. It is a place in which there is no hierarchy of persons (although there is probably a hierarchy in roles). Each person within such an open culture is of equal worth – each is a child of God. A Church ministry that develops a culture of dialogue and mutual listening pays equal respect to each member. It is a place where there is no gender divide, no ethnic divide, no divide because of qualifications and background, no rich and poor. It is the Church Paul spoke of in Galatians 3:28-29. It is a Church that honours the *sensus fidei* of the whole People of God.

Dialogue and mutual listening are fundamentally different from the benevolent consultation of a ruler listening to subjects. A culture of dialogue and mutual listening creates 'spaces of grace' for discussion, dissonance and diversity of opinion, all conducted freely because members have confidence that there is a mutuality of respect within those spaces. We should not be surprised that there are still areas in the Church where this freedom and mutuality of respect are absent. Where this occurs, the consequence can be a culture of fear that hinders creativity in mission because employees know questioning, disagreement or alternate suggestions are not tolerated. On the other hand, attention to faithful dissent can lead to creative dialogue that serves the greater common good. When the voice that is different – be it strident or quiet – is marginalised, it can come at a high cost for the individuals concerned *and* the overall mission outcomes.

How will those in governance build a culture where women, men, young, old, poor, wealthy, inexperienced and experienced know they are respected and know their voice is as important as anyone else's? And beyond the confines of a given ministry, what measures will leaders create for ecumenical engagement and for listening to our society? A culture of dialogue, mutual listening and discernment is a powerful tool in developing a creative mission-oriented focus.

### (iii) A synodal Church acts in a spirit of service

The spirit of service in governance embraces a sense of stewardship, a commitment to transparency, ethical behaviour, and integrity that leads naturally towards a culture of humility, simplicity and an orientation to the 'other'.

A culture of stewardship implies accountability based on respect for the various stakeholders involved. Stewardship implies a culture across the whole ministry of acting on behalf of a community of stakeholders. It recalls the leadership discussed in Chapter 5 that does not act for its own intentions but for the common good and for the 'other'. In health, for example, this community of stakeholders might include patients; patients' families; health researchers and professionals; as well as the founding religious institute, the larger 'other' of all Catholic health institutions; and even, at times, national health institutions. For all ministries, stewardship includes acting as stewards of creation, stewards of the future of our earth.[17] Consequently we must understand how stewardship of creation and stewardship for the future are built into a governance agenda?

Expressions of accountability and stewardship are found when there is clarity regarding the authority vested in respective roles in a given ministry, or area of ministry – when there are clear processes for reporting, monitoring and follow-up. For example, a parish demonstrates stewardship and accountability, not only when it makes careful use of the funds donated by parishioners but when it discusses the allocation and deployment of those funds openly with parishioners. A summary statement that simply gives the bottom line of income, expenditure, assets and commitments is less than adequate. While some parishioners will be interested in less detail than others, all parishioners deserve the option to see full details of expenditure and planned budgets for future allocations. Stewardship applies to all resources – financial, physical, human, environmental, cultural, spiritual, and the future.

Good stewardship has nothing to hide. It is at the service of the larger community and is transparent in its actions. Transparent governance breeds an openness. It allows those outside the circle of governing to see clearly through windows into the governing processes and operations. Transparent governance welcomes dialogue with stakeholders and the wider community because that is part of the ethos of service. When governance within the Church has been seen as less than transparent, this has rightly earned rebuke and loss of credibility from society at large. It has also disenfranchised many faithful within the Church community. An element of transparency is open communication. For example, if there is a change in parish priest, how is that communicated? By whom? If the change is fraught perhaps because it has been precipitated by necessary disciplinary action, there is even more reason for parishioners to receive appropriate and timely information.

Good stewardship honours integrity in its service. A culture of ethical behaviour implies at its most basic level a compliance with civil and canonical law. Other aspects of ethical behaviour involve truth-telling, probity, fidelity.[18] We can also use 'ethical' (in the sense of integrity) to describe faithfulness, not only to the letter of the law, but to the spirit of the gospel and consistency with the teachings of Jesus. If we learn nothing else from the scandals of sexual abuse of children in our Church, we must learn that we cannot presume that we – ourselves and others – will always act with integrity. The 'we' includes leaders at all levels in the Church.

We must live mindful of our capacity for sin. In practical ways, a lack of integrity can follow from the temptation towards privileging ourselves if we are in leadership positions. Self-delusion in this regard can include: 'I am a Principal and I'm working really long hours, so I deserve to have this perk' (from the school budget). Or, 'Everyone knows I'm doing a great job as Director. I don't need to go through an appraisal like the rest of my staff.' 'I'm ordained. That (rule/expectation) doesn't apply to me.'

Where does abuse of people start? Where does abuse of property and resources start? It starts with the first small infringement after someone gives themselves the privilege of seeing themselves as somehow being different, someone above others, someone marked out and for whom exception is permitted. Integrity doesn't ask what is allowed but what is right? Thus we must ask, what will be the guidelines that institutional leaders set for themselves in terms of a humble and simple style in their operation?

### (iv) A synodal Church is a Church open to conversion and to the urging of the Spirit.

Governance that is open to 'invasions' and 'irruptions' of the Spirit is governance by cultural leaders who pay attention to their interior life. Such leaders will situate their discernment and decision-making within a spirit of prayer and reflection. This is part of the search for 'being us at our best' as discussed in Chapter 5. In our experience, this is a well-established practice in Church ministries. In addition to such reflective discernment, other aspects of a Church open to conversion can include institutional cultures that welcome critique; an openness and humility to reflect upon what is and to seek advice on what might be; and an attitude of conversion. There will always be gaps in the practice and ways we as individuals and agencies serve our shared mission. We shouldn't be unduly surprised by our inadequacies. That is all part of being a pilgrim Church, people on the way, a Church both holy and broken. Putting our trust in God, we can acknowledge our brokenness and move on.

It is for those in governance to determine the structures that might reflect a mission that is always open to the Spirit's guidance, the processes that facilitate an acknowledgement of inadequacies and mistakes, and ways to improve service to those who are the focus of a given area of ministry. For example, some ministries (especially those in the area of health and education) regularly invite formal review of their performance against their mission mandate, their priorities and the structures in place to promote mission. (We will discuss the issue of personal critique and review in the following chapter.)

One inspiring example of this commitment to good governance through critique comes from the small Catholic community in the Diocese of Tonga and Niue, a community that is sprawled across islands in the Pacific. In 2013, the Director of Catholic Education, with the support of his Bishop and Diocesan School Board, instigated a comprehensive review of the total school system, precisely to appraise its alignment with mission and identify ongoing priorities. There were no surplus funds to complete this task. (In fact, the Diocese and its school system

were struggling financially.) However, the Diocesan leaders were so committed to a serious critique of the education ministry, that they engaged the two authors of this as external consultants, and raised the necessary funds for the review from the expatriate communities in the USA, New Zealand and Australia. The outcomes of the review have been vigorously adopted by the Cardinal and Director and have shaped subsequent and future directions in Catholic education in the diocese.

### (v) A synodal Church works as community in processes of shared decision-making, based on the *sensus fidei* of the People of God

A Church agency that works as community in shared decision-making creates a culture that is participatory, collaborative, inclusive and discerning. Embedded in this culture is an attentiveness to the *sensus fidei* and an understanding of subsidiarity.

Such a culture can be promoted through the establishment of appropriate structures (or tools) for participation, mutual dialogue and listening for discernment. For example, at the whole-of-Church level in Australia, the Plenary Council process has attempted an exercise in consultation and reflection. Despite the limitations of the Plenary Council (because of Canon Law strictures about a hierarchical-heavy participation), we recognise the step it represents towards a more participatory culture in the governance of the Australian Church.

Archbishop Costelloe, in his paper on 'Discernment' in preparation for the Plenary, signalled that the process of discernment that was begun in 2018 will not be complete with the Council event, but will be an ongoing process of unfolding at local levels.[19] This is encouraging, especially if it means that processes of listening to the faithful continue as a mode of discernment and decision-making in the Church. National discernment and shared decision-making on the scale of the Plenary might be reasonably infrequent. However, regular cycles of consultation and discernment at parish, deanery and diocesan levels are simple to initiate and should be normative in a synodal Church. When the Plenary process was initiated in Australia, one elderly Catholic observed: 'This is the first time in my life as a Catholic that anyone has asked me what I hope for my Church.' We should all hope never to hear that said again.

A good example of creating structures that express a synodal Church lies in those dioceses that have established consultative Pastoral Councils at diocesan and deanery levels as well as at parish level. Like any new venture, there will be learning along the way in how these Pastoral Councils can best operate. Already there are some that are moving forward in a mission-oriented, listening, joint decision-making mode. They should be encouraged by the words of Pope Francis when addressing members of diocesan pastoral councils in Assisi in 2013. After welcoming and thanking the assembly of pastoral council members, he exclaimed, 'How needed pastoral councils are! A bishop cannot guide a diocese without pastoral councils. A parish priest cannot guide the parish without the parish council. This is fundamental!'[20]

Yet these initiatives have value only if – and only when – they are inclusive in the widest understanding of the term. Inclusion means creating places at decision-making tables for women as well as men, for young and old, for those from diverse ethnic groups served by a ministry, for the Indigenous as well as the more recent arrival, for those with a disability, for the poor as well as those who are well-off, for parents as well as single people, for the happily married as well as those who are in other stages of relationship, for LGBTIQ+ alike. We will not rehearse the arguments for the importance of women being included in significant governance roles in Church ministries. It is ironic that the Church lags so far behind a consciousness of this, which is now prevailing in the commercial and public spheres. If we as Church were being true to our prophetic self, we would be leading the way.

By and large, despite much rhetoric, this characteristic of inclusivity and collaboration in decision-making (and broader governance) remains one of the stumbling blocks of Church governance. One of the greatest obstacles to developing a participatory, collaborative and inclusive culture around decision-making can be the mindset of leaders. Especially at the parish level, this has impeded the potential of Parish Pastoral Councils.

In 1965 – nearly 60 years ago – the Vatican wrote: 'In dioceses, as far as possible, councils should be set up to assist the Church's apostolic work, whether in the field of making the gospel known and people holy, or in charitable, social or other spheres.'[21] While there are exceptions and outstanding examples of this to date, Diocesan and Parish Pastoral Councils that are pastorally-focused, collaborative, transparent mission-oriented councils of discernment – remain some of the least-realised of the structures for mission proposed by Vatican II in Australia.[22]

Setting an example for all ministries, some Parish Pastoral Councils set aside quality time each year to go away to a desert place together; they spend time in prayer and *communio*; they break bread together and discern priorities and actions for the community for the year ahead. This is not a group of parishioners 'helping' Father, but a group of parish leaders reflecting together on mission. This is one way a synodal Church might act. Another example is the way some parish teams – Parish Priest, Pastoral Associate, and others with responsibilities, (for example sacramental, youth coordinators and school leaders) work together as a team, rather than as individuals. When they do, they make possible a greater sharing of the talents and wisdom of those involved, leading to possibilities beyond the imagination of a Parish Priest alone, or a Pastoral Associate alone. A by-product of this approach is that in itself it is educational and transformative. By being engaged in the process of discerning mission directions and priorities, everyone on the parish ministerial team is invited into leadership for mission. Certainly this may be messy – perhaps taking more time than a Parish Leader might desire – nonetheless such a journey together is another face of a synodal community of faith. Consequently, there are many such examples of good practice across ministries in Australia.

## Conclusion

Structures, direction-setting, planning, policy and reporting and accountability – the work of good governance – need to align, and be seen to align, coherently with the vision, values and principles of an organisation. It can be a Rubik's cube of complexity, balancing vision and mission with an appropriate mode of governance in the context of professional demands and organisational circumstances, but such alignment is critically important.

The building of a synodal culture in Church ministries cannot be left to chance. It follows then that the selection, development and support of leaders for those ministries must become a priority. Investment in the development and learning of leaders – those entrusted with this aspect of carrying forward the mission – is a critical part of governance and ensuring the right people are in the right places in the Church's ministries.

### Activity 6.1: Messages about culture

Consider your agency/ministry in the light of the Reinforcing Mechanisms listed by Robins and Decenzo in Chapter 3:

1. Community design and structure.
2. Community systems and procedures.
3. Rites, rituals and ceremonies of the community.
4. Design of physical space, facades, and buildings.
5. Stories about important events and people.
6. Formal statements of community's philosophy, creeds, and charters.

What are the messages about your area of work that these cultural indicators might give to a complete stranger?

## Endnotes

1. GPPT, LSC, 5
2. Robert Fitzgerald, Foreword, *GBOM*, p. 3.
3. It is not within the scope of this book to explore the details of Canon Law relating to governance of pastoral agencies. However, it is pertinent to note that some rulings appear very limited in terms of synodality.
4. See for example, Public Sector Governance, https://www.apsc.gov.au/building-better-governance; Pearse Trust, The Core Principles Of Good Corporate Governance, 19 Feb 2014, https://www.pearse-trust.ie/blog/bid/108866/the-core-principles-of-good-corporate-governance; Governance Institute of Australia, Governance foundations, https://www.governanceinstitute.com.au/resources/what-is-governance/governance-foundations/ accessed 7th May 2020; Susan Pascoe, Best Practice in Governance of Church Agencies, Keynote Address delivered to the Principles and Practice for Church Governance Conference, (Melbourne: Yarra Theological Union and University of Divinity, 2019) accessed 9 June, 2020, https://www.ampjps.org.au/wp-content/uploads/2019/03/Pascoe-Best-Practice-in-Governance-YTU-3Mar2019.pdf; David Ranson, Theology of Church Governance, Paper presented to the Principles and Practice of Church Governance Workshop, (Melbourne 2-3 March 2019); Lawrie Hallinan, Governance as mission and opportunity for collaboration, Workshop within the Mission: One Heart, Many Voices Conference, 14 May 2019.
5. Robert Fitzgerald, *GBOM*, p. 3.
6. Pope Francis, Letter to the Pilgrim People of God in Germany, 29 June 2019, #5.
7. Pope Francis, 2019, #5.
8. Pope Francis, 2019, #3.
9. GRPT, LSC, p. 38.
10. Final Document, Amazonian Synod, #88. Cf. Chapter 4 of this text.
11. Pope Francis, Address to the Participants of the World Congress, Educating Today and Tomorrow. A Renewing Passion. November 21, 2015.
12. Pope Francis, Homily, Chrism Mass, St Peter's Basilica, 28 March 2013.
13. For example, Anne Benjamin, Taking the next step: Catholic schools and the cry of the poor in A. Benjamin & D. Riley Eds, *Catholic Schools. Hope in Uncertain Times*. John Garratt Publishing, Melbourne, 2008, pp. 192-206.
14. Pope Francis, World Congress on Education, 2015.
15. Chapter 2.
16. It is interesting to visit the websites of different dioceses, parishes, PJPs, education, health and welfare agencies. Some are inspiring, welcoming and gospel-focused; some are dull and uninviting and could be those of a commercial corporation.
17. Cf. Pope Francis, *Laudato si*.
18. Cf *LSC* 46
19. Archbishop Timothy Costelloe SDB, A Journey of Discernment, the Plenary Council, August 2020.
20. Pope Francis, Address, Meeting with members of diocesan pastoral councils, 4 October 2013, http://www.vatican.va/content/francesco/en/speeches/2013/october/documents/papa-francesco_20131004_clero-assisi.html
21. Vatican II, *Decree on the Apostolate of Lay People*, #26
22. See LSC, Section 6.11.7 and Appendix 3, reporting on a Governance in Australia Survey 2019 that revealed that only 10 of 30 dioceses responding to the survey had Diocesan Pastoral Councils.

# Chapter 7
# People in Leadership

If the role of good governance is to drive the mission and ethos forward, the critical drivers of this, as discussed in Chapter 3, are the leaders. Some scholars even suggest that creating and managing culture is the 'only thing of real importance' that leaders do.[1] This is nicely summarised by Catholics for Renewal when they emphasise that 'good governance is also dependent on good leadership and shared culture which ensure that all in the organisation are committed to the organisation's mission'.[2]

In the creation of a culture that promotes the mission of the Church, one of the most important responsibilities in governance is ensuring that the right people are in the right positions to facilitate the alignment of operations, culture and mission. The 'right people' in this context means leaders with the mindset, skills and formation that will promote synodality. Consequently, in this chapter we will focus on the people in ministerial leadership and organisational practices with respect to those who are leaders.

It is self-evident that a culture that reflects a synodal Church is more likely to be promoted when leaders: are able to work, and choose to work, in a way that is participatory, collaborative and inclusive; when they demonstrate a commitment to reflection, critique and transparency; and if they are mission-oriented community-builders. A synodal Church needs leaders who can work within these parameters and consciously work to strengthen them. No one is expected to be everything; each of us has limitations and strengths and that is the joy of working collaboratively. A more synodal Church is unlikely without synodal leaders. In other words, leadership in the Church suggests certain qualities of its leaders.

A starting point is leaders who cherish the synodal character of Church and the corollary, understanding that being Church equals being synodal, that is, one that is mission-oriented in its response to pastoral challenges, develops a culture of inclusion, dialogue and mutual listening, acts in a spirit of service, and is open to conversion and to the urging of the Spirit. Also, such leaders work as a part of a community in processes of shared decision-making, implying that appropriate leaders in ministry are those who have the skills and aptitude for fostering such a Church.

This presumes that those chosen for leadership in the Church value exercising leadership in relationship – (i) in relationship in the communion of disciples, (ii) in relationship with the mission entrusted to the Church, (iii) in relationship with those we serve, and (iv) in relationship with those with whom we serve.

Earlier we noted that how leaders view power, influence and authority as important elements in the culture they develop. We noted too that the influence of leaders rests in the relationships they have with the people they serve, especially those with the least power.[3] Pope Francis's comments in the TED talk previously quoted build on this. Speaking of tenderness as the choice of the most courageous, he highlighted the significance of a leader's influence, stressing 'the more powerful you are, the more your actions will have an impact on people, the more responsible you are to act humbly. If you don't, your power will ruin you, and will ruin the other'.[4]

As with governance, good administrative structures, processes and practices within an organisation – especially those relating to an organisation's people – are at the service of the mission. Ideally, they should make it easier for those who are engaged in a given ministry to exercise their role to the best of their ability and for the good of the whole ministry. Administration in all its phases requires constant discernment and critique against the measure to which it assists women and men in a given area of ministry to progress their mission. Not all organisational processes are consistent with the mission and culture of a synodal Church. Not all cultures are life-giving. Some can be obstacles, even a scandal. Governance, administration and culture work together to promote the mission and values – or rub against the mission and values to produce dissonance, lack of authenticity and lack of credibility.

## Sustaining leaders through organisational support

While leadership in a synodal Church assumes certain qualities in a leader, those in these positions are entitled to expect support for their leadership through appropriate preparation, induction, ongoing support, feedback, affirmation and oversight.

For senior leaders in the Church, we assume that these elements are provided within a collegial system of relationships, dialogue, discernment and other processes that enable them to enhance their leadership for a synodal Church. For other leaders, responsibility for organisational support rests with both the leader and their supervisor. Let us share a story...

> A young woman who had been cradled in Catholicism was about 30 when, in the wake of Vatican II and

its promises, she developed a conviction about the importance of education in faith with adult Catholics. Following post-graduate study in Religious Education overseas, she persuaded her diocese to create a role for this purpose. She was given a desk in a 100-year-old school building along with two Sisters of St Joseph who worked with religious education teachers in primary and secondary schools, and a family of pigeons whose presence became unavoidably obvious whenever a strong sea breeze rattled around under the ancient slate roof.

In O'Meara's terms, she assumed a public activity on behalf of the community. It was generally typical of that time that there was no formal letter of appointment, no formal commissioning, no role statement, no ongoing oversight, no performance review. From time to time she asked to meet with her employer to report on what she was doing, and she prepared a written report each year. There was little, ongoing feedback on her performance – virtually none – and most of the time she was left to her own devices.

She recalls these years in her life as difficult and lonely ones. While some clergy welcomed her role and her efforts, others were hostile, even discourteous. Inclusion was not on the agenda. The role ended badly. With hindsight and experience, she acknowledges there were strategies she might have initiated in support of her work. For example, she could have ensured that the Diocesan Education Board and the Senate of priests and pastors were better briefed and more formally involved; or she might have requested a formally-convened advisory committee for adult religious education, which (especially in the absence of other structures and leadership from her employer), could have provided some supervision of her work, monitored its quality, given feedback, advised on strategic direction, clarified and defined the role, and acted as an advocate for the ministry of adult education. She was inexperienced, pretty much alone and not wise enough to think of these things.

That would have been around the late 1970s – a long time ago. The ministries of education, health and welfare, overall have, in the intervening years, developed highly sophisticated organisations with much demonstration of very good employee-services practice. Organisational support generally, and for those in pastoral ministry, has come a long way. At the parish level, especially, a great deal has been achieved. However, gaps in good practice remain. Of concern in recent years have been those dioceses that seem to have abandoned these carefully developed processes, thereby jeopardising sound organisational practice, along with transparency. Such an approach brings the double disadvantage of doing a disservice to the individuals concerned while not maximising the potential benefit for mission.

## Supporting leaders in a synodal Church

In the remainder of this chapter, we will work through some ways in which a synodal Church culture might appropriately look after and work with its employees, with a focus on leadership. (This book makes no claim to be a general text on all aspects of an organisation.) We have selected seven areas that pertain to people in organisations.

i. Preparation for leadership

ii. Recruitment and selection

iii. Induction & ongoing supervision

iv. Ongoing professional development

v. Performance review

vi. Sustaining leadership and leadership succession

vii. Separation.

We will not focus on these as human resource processes per se, but as instruments for promoting the culture of synodality we have been exploring in previous chapters. As noted earlier, an organisation's values and beliefs need to be embedded into its culture if the core mission is to be realised and its activities seen to be authentic. With the lens for consideration being that of a synodal Church, our methodology will be to nominate selected questions in each area for consideration by those responsible for shaping policy and practice in different Church agencies and organisations.

### i. Preparation for leadership

In what ways can the preparation of leaders equip them for ministry in a synodal Church?

As stated previously the Church is synodal by its nature and origins: it is a communion of witnesses to the Word: in relationship with Christ and with others: called for the sake of its mission to adopt a relational manner 'that places emphasis on listening, welcoming, dialogue and common discernment in a process that transforms the lives of those taking part'[5]; all under the guidance of the Holy Spirit.

Our society regulates most professions, trades and businesses with expectations about preparation and qualifications for the services being offered. We do not expect to go to an untrained dentist. Either situation would be unwise and unfair. Likewise, it is only wise and fair that those appointed to positions of responsibility in the Church are trained and supported for their role. While some individuals show a natural talent for something we commonly recognise as leadership, it is not a magical domain: there are theories and practices that can be studied that enhances an individual's capacity to conceptualise their role of leadership and apply it in practice.

To be leaders in such a Church presumes an understanding of Church as synodal; skills in listening, welcoming, dialogue and shared discernment; and, most critically, an attitude that is predisposed towards such a way of being and leading Church. This applies not only to those employed for leadership in a ministry, but also those who voluntarily assume leadership roles, such as those on pastoral councils, school boards and other governing bodies.

Taking the example of pastoral ministry, how can the education of priests prepare them for such a role of leadership? It is not the role of parish priests to do things for parishioners, wonderful, creative and pastoral as these initiatives may be. Rather, it is their role to work with parishioners to support them in their living out of their baptismal mission. One parish priest expressed it this way:

> The mark of true leadership is not telling people what to do, but being able to bring people with you, all heading together with a common goal. And for that, one needs to be able to relate to a whole range of people, in a relaxed and confident way.[6]

The parish does not belong to the parish priest: it is a community of *laos* together – priest and people – that he has been appointed to serve in leading worship, evangelising, pastoral service and the facilitation of parishioners' living out their mission. Pope Benedict XVI spoke of the necessity 'to improve pastoral structures in such a way that the co-responsibility of all the members of the People of God in their entirety is gradually promoted'. He added that this 'demands a change in mindset, particularly concerning lay people. They must no longer be viewed as "collaborators" of the clergy but truly recognised as "co-responsible" for the Church's being and action, thereby fostering the consolidation of a mature and committed laity'.[7]

In exploring effective priestly ministry over a number of years, the Boston Seminar was an interesting project involving female and male theologians. The final report, 'To Serve the People of God,' highlights five essential characteristics for effective priestly ministry:

a) the capacity to preach the word of God in ways that nurture the faith, hope, and love of the disciples of Christ

b) the ability to lead the Christian community in life-enhancing prayer and worship

c) the willingness and aptitude to be a collaborative leader among lay ecclesial ministers and the whole people of God

d) the disposition to lead an exemplary life of discipleship within the ecclesial community

e) the commitment to practise pastoral charity in service of the gospel.[8]

The discussion above has focused on just one of these, 'the willingness and aptitude to be a collaborative leader', but each one of the five characteristics is nuanced and deliberate, demanding attention in a contemporary preparation for ordained ministry.

Likewise, the model of transrelational leadership offers further possibilities for conceptualising leadership that fosters the relational elements of synodality. This sits happily with the conclusion of Archbishop Coleridge who, following the *Meeting on the Protection of Minors in the Church* in Rome in February 2019, was widely reported as saying preparation for priesthood needed to be re-designed and that 'attempts to tweak' the existing model were unlikely to succeed; and that the Church

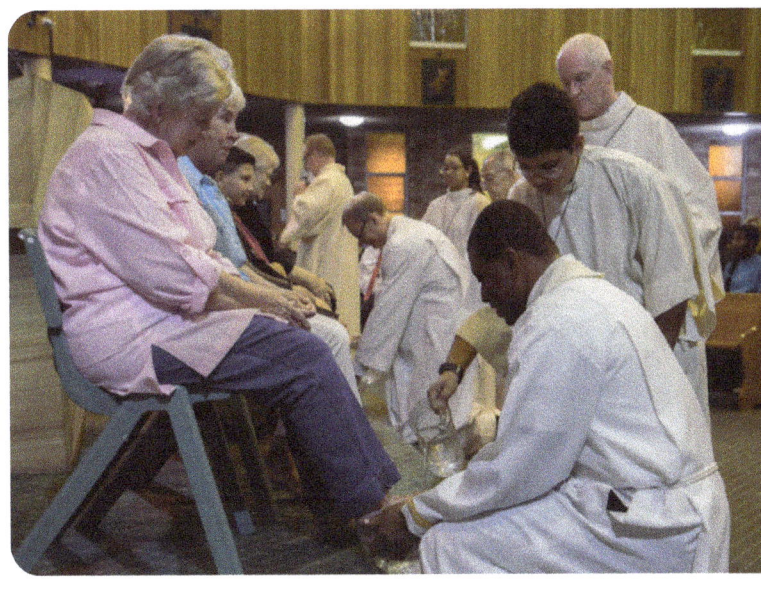

needed to 'seriously consider an institute of Church leadership, where the presbyters are trained and formed, but with others as well, so that all forms of Church leadership would be part of this institute'.[9] In a later chapter we outline a suggested framework for leadership development in which all those preparing for leadership in a ministry learn together.

While the Boston Seminar, and the previous paragraphs, concentrated on ordained ministry, most, if not all of the characteristics, can be applied to preparation for all leaders in pastoral ministry.[10]

### ii. Recruitment and selection of leaders

- Are there professional processes in place for the recruitment and selection of leaders for different roles in the Church?

- Do policies and practices enshrine a commitment that leadership roles reflect the diversity of the Church – male and female, age, ethnicity, etc?

- Are there clear role statements for those leading a ministry in the Church, and do these explicitly reflect characteristics of a synodal Church?

These are just some sample questions pertinent to the important area of recruiting leaders for a ministry. The answer to all three is probably a resounding 'Yes' and an equally resounding 'No'. That is, professional practices in identifying leaders are unevenly implemented across the various ministries in the Australian Church. On the positive side, they are much better than they were.

Good practice in these areas is more likely to yield good results for all concerned. We have observed a standard rule in recruitment: bad beginnings lead to bad outcomes. 'Bad' beginnings include the scarcity or absence of open, transparent and systematic processes. For example, a senior Church leader chooses a recruitment agency on the basis of the person being a friend, rather than obtaining a formal proposal and competitive quotation; or a senior leader simply appoints someone to a leadership position, without any normally accepted processes of recruitment. Further along the scale of 'bad' is the removal of a competent incumbent so that a preferred person might be installed instead, with no appropriate processes (for example, of review, contract renewal or recruitment). It is a concern when these and similar poor practices are reported as still occurring in the 2020 Australian Church. Apart from being open, transparent, ethical and accountable to the community – all hallmarks of good governance – professional recruitment processes allow for a broader range of candidates to present themselves, candidates who might be far better suitable than one personally appointed. This enriches the potential of the role into the future. Similarly, a candidate who has earned a position has a far different attitude from one who has had it given to them. This can potentially create a dangerous relationship of indebtedness and patronage when a person is appointed directly outside normal open processes.

Even though education and health ministries generally have highly developed sound practices regarding employment, we have been surprised to discover recently that some Diocesan Directors of Education have not had written role statements. A benign Bishop might say, in words, or their (in)-actions might imply, 'That's fine. X is a very competent person. I have every confidence in them. They know they're in charge of the schools. That's all they need.' No, Bishop. It is not. And you need more also. So does the Director. So do other stakeholders.

The same principle applies across all leadership roles. Not all Pastoral Workers in parishes and those who lead some diocesan ministries (e.g. youth) have clear role statements, or they sometimes have role statements that, taken literally, would require them to work a 14-day week. Do Pastoral Council members – parish, deanery or diocesan – have a clear understanding of their role before they accept nomination? Do they have a clear understanding of the respective responsibilities of Members, Chair and others (e.g. Parish Priest, Dean, Bishop)?

Neglecting specific definition of the beginning and end of any leader's responsibilities and authority simply sets both the employer and the leader up for possible misunderstandings; it provides no clarity for the leader and her/his delegations; it provides no frame of reference for feedback on the leader's performance, both positive and negative, thus leaving contract renewal processes a matter of 'a wink and a nod' or a 'goodbye' from the employer (with or without a thank you').

Routine formalities such as role statements can sharpen the focus of an individual's efforts, protect employees, and make life easier for their employers. Included in this clearly defined statement of expectations should also be clarity about reporting. To whom? When? This is something, surprisingly, that is not always clear. And, of course, they should link each role directly to the mission being served.

### iii. Induction and ongoing supervision

- What support is in place for those newly appointed to leadership roles in the Church?

- What processes of induction are planned to initiate them into either a particular organisation or role?
- How are experienced leaders coming from other contexts (e.g. priests from overseas) inducted into the culture and circumstances of their new role?
- Are there briefings on the particular history, culture and existing priorities of the place of ministry (school, department, institution, parish)?
- What processes are in place for full briefing on matters of ethics, values and compliance (e.g. National Catholic Safeguarding Standards[11], amongst others)?
- Is there provision for ongoing coaching and peer-to-peer mentoring for less-experienced leaders, including leaders coming from other cultures and contexts (e.g. from the commercial sector to a Church ministry; from public service to education, welfare or health)?

Induction and ongoing support apply not only to those entering into roles such as Parish Priest, Diocesan or Parish Youth/Sacramental Coordinator, Head of Department, Principal, Director and Trustee, but also to those involved in other decision-making and consultative bodies. That is, after initial preparation and selection, members of Boards, Parish Pastoral Councils, Deanery Pastoral Councils, Diocesan Pastoral Councils, and even Diocesan Consultants deserve to be supported in their mandate of co-responsibility in the Church, through appropriate conversation about how they exercise their role and what would assist them to do so in the spirit of a Vatican II Church. Special attention should be paid to those in leadership roles that, by definition, are fairly solitary, such as some diocesan roles are. There are excellent examples of these roles across the Catholic Church in Australia and overseas as well as other Christian traditions.[12]

*A senior educator reported that early in his role in the education office he worked with a team of former principals who reported to him. Each of these Principal Consultants was responsible for overseeing a cluster of schools for quality education, compliance, coaching and support. After a few months, one of these highly experienced principals asked the senior educator: 'How am I going? You never give me any feedback.' The senior educator was stopped in his tracks. He had been delighted with the Principal Consultant's work but hadn't let him know. He had assumed that because the Consultant was experienced and competent, he didn't need feedback. He was wrong!*

'Supervision' simply means someone offering a larger perspective, a helicopter-view, and discernment of a situation. Supervision can encompass coaching, monitoring, guiding, directing, correcting, developing – all as appropriate. Such ongoing assistance can provide for those in any position of leadership an important support that flows on to building the wellbeing of the communities in which people serve. It can also help build the capacity of those working in a leadership role, whether it is in a parish team, a diocesan office, a school, a hospital or another agency.

### iv. Performance Review

- Do the policies and practices of the (diocese, parish, schools office, health department, welfare agency, etc.) enshrine a commitment to performance review of all those in formal roles in the organisation as an expression of transparency, an opportunity to acknowledge formally the achievements of individuals in their roles, and accountability to the community and to the Church's mission?
- What evidence is there of measures of accountability for all those in formal roles, ordained and commissioned (e.g. through performance reviews, reporting to community and calling to account)?

Church agencies, such as those in education, health and welfare, are familiar with the processes of good administration and leadership. Such processes include accountability and ongoing learning, and this was reinforced by the findings of the Royal Commission into Institutional Responses to Child Sexual Abuse. However, the Commission went on to add that:

> We heard that the Catholic Church in Australia has developed a code of conduct for clergy and religious that includes standards in relation to professional development, professional supervision and appraisal. However, we also heard that most clergy do not fully comply with ongoing formation activities.[13]

It would probably be news to most Catholics to read that there are such standards for professional development, professional supervision and appraisal of clergy in Australia. Other Christian traditions likewise face the challenge of introducing and implementing appropriate processes of support, supervision and accountability for their leaders. The Lutheran Church of Australia, for example, has well-articulated policies of review for their bishops, including the National Bishop, as well as for their clergy and others in pastoral ministry. Not unexpectedly, there are some issues with implementation that the Lutherans are grappling with. Sharing such experiences could be mutually useful.

Appraisal (or some form of review) is not merely a tool of accountability to the community on whose behalf a leader serves, and not merely a measure of transparency to that community, but it is also a valuable opportunity for the leader to receive feedback and affirmation on his/her exercise of leadership, guidance on future priorities in that leadership and provision of tailored professional assistance (e.g.

through formal learning, directed reading, coaching, and other experiences) to support that leadership.

### v. Ongoing professional development

- Do the policies and practices (of the diocese, parish, schools' office, health department, welfare agency, etc.) enshrine a commitment to ongoing professional learning for all those in ordained and in other formal roles in the diocese as expression of openness to learning?
- What opportunities for professional development are provided? Where are gaps in skills across individuals and teams?
- Is there a budget for ongoing professional learning and who knows what it is?
- Is there a clear process for accessing ongoing professional development and who knows about it?
- How does the leadership honour their commitment to offer enculturation in ethos for a ministry while respecting the individual belief and meaning system of each staff member?

One of the most critical means of sustaining leadership, we are convinced, is through ongoing professional learning and reflection, especially through development at various levels. Our experience is that ongoing professional learning and reflection sustain the depth, richness and conviction of those in leadership, just as being part of a community of shared faith and mutual regard sustains the heart of a ministry. In conjunction with regular performance reviews, ongoing learning can, in theological terms, provide moments of grace, moments of conversion.

Professional learning also occurs in a powerful way when individuals or groups of individuals reflect in depth on their experiences, challenges and responses. A commitment to ongoing professional learning, and resourcing of such learning, has been well-embedded in education ministries. Some excellent examples of this include: a program for women on maternity leave to enable them to keep in touch with their workplace and to complete professional development (at reduced cost) even while on leave; provision for job-sharing; mentoring for principals beginning their principalship and also for women considering leadership; work-life balance practices; provision for principals to take three days a year for a retreat; networks for the exchange of learning; spiritual formation and counselling provision for all staff.

Everyone who is engaged by the Church in a ministry is entitled to expect opportunities for ongoing learning, for ongoing development that will help them to reflect on their understanding, and expand and deepen their skills, for the sake of 'making God and his Incarnate Son present and in a sense visible'. In this, everyone means everyone: Pastoral Associates, Youth and Sacramental Coordinators, Pastoral Council members, Board members.

Such learning can occur in a variety of forms (e.g., formal study, short courses, time for formal guided reading, exchange visits to similar ministries, attendance at conferences/seminars, coaching, etc.). Resourcing such learning does not mean breaking the organisation's bank. However, a budget provision for ongoing professional development is a good indicator that this is on the leader's agenda. In a synodal, reflective pilgrim Church, in constant processes of conversion and renewal, openness to learning can be one way of expressing an openness to the Spirit.

### vi. Separation

- What rituals are there where a person completes their time of service in a Church agency?
- Whatever the reason for leaving, is each person farewelled with respect for the service they have offered?

We have seen some ungodly separations. No divorce could be as cruel or painful as the dehumanising and disrespectful way some leaders and other employees have departed their roles without acknowledgement and without due process. And this in a Church that espouses a founder famed for his compassion and a Church which proclaims respect for each person as reflecting the likeness of God. Again, this has been an area that, in our experience, has generally involved courtesy and graciousness in educational agencies, where the service and contribution of individuals has been respected and honoured. Unfortunately, we have observed in recent years that even such well-established good practice can be eroded when the culture of leadership changes.

### vii. Sustaining Leadership and Succession planning

- What strategies are in place to sustain leadership in the ((diocese, parish, school, agency, ministry)?
- What strategies are in place to develop new generations of leadership in the (diocese, parish, school, agency, ministry)?
- How is the learning and experience of existing and previous leaders passed on the new generations?

There are two sides to this. One is the organisational initiative required to support current leaders and to identify and prepare the next generation. The other resides in the actions of the individual leader to sustain herself/himself in their role of leadership, whether they see it as an exercise of discipleship for the Kingdom, or in other terms.

## Conclusion

The leaders in any organisation play a critical role in the effectiveness of the culture of that organisation. Through their discernment, they can enable or can inhibit those entrusted with carrying out the mission and vision of an organisation; they can clarify the articulation between vision and action or they can obfuscate it; they can promote a culture that is in harmony with the mission or provide a sign of contradiction; they can enliven and encourage innovation and creativity or they can dampen enthusiasm with wet blankets of regulation, precedent and excessive caution; they can invite staff to develop their leadership capacity or they can shrivel this capacity, especially through lack of meaningful and equitable participation of women and men. In their leadership, they are called to witness to who we are called to be as followers of Jesus Christ. Next, we will propose a model of leadership as a process of moral discernment.

### Activity 7.1

You might invite your team to read this chapter and identify which questions are of significance to the team's present situation. List any actions that might be necessary or appropriate.

## Endnotes

1. Schein, quoted in Chapter 3.
2. GBOM, p.111.
3. Quoting Michel Foucault.
4. Pope Francis, TED Talk.
5. Synod on Youth, #122.
6. Crothers, p. 61.
7. Pope Benedict XVI, 2009. The 2020 'Instruction on the parish' from the Vatican might seem to contradict this view from the Emeritus Pope, but it is probably more accurate to see in the 'Instruction' another example of the juxtaposition of different ecclesiologies jostling each other in the one document as different parts of the institutional Church catch up with each other.
8. Boston Seminar.
9. Archbishop Mark Coleridge, Interview with Joshua J. McElwee, 'Archbishop suggests creating new Vatican office to tackle abuse, clerical culture', National Catholic Reporter, February 22, 2019. https://www.ncronline.org/print/news/accountability/exclusive-archbishop-suggests-creating-new-vatican-office-tackle-abuse-clerical
10. Some significant issues relating to preparation for ministry have been documented by Bishop Geoffrey Robinson, for example, in Petition to Rome, 2013; 'Advice to Bishops on Royal Commission,' Eureka St, 16 November, 2012, https://www.eurekastreet.com.au/article/advice-to-bishops-on-royal-commission
11. Catholic Professional Standards Ltd, National Catholic Safeguarding Standards, Edition 1, 2019, https://www.cpsltd.org.au/safe-church/national-catholic-safeguarding-standards/
12. There are many examples of good pastoral practice cited in LSC, Section 7. Others include, for example, Australian Catholic Bishops Conference, Faithful Stewards of God's Grace. Lay Pastoral Ministers in the Church in Australia, July 2018; Aengus Kavanagh, ed, A Call to Re-set the Sails, Plenary Council 2020, Patrician Brothers, 2020; Robert Dixon, Jane McMahon, Stephen Reid, George Keryk, Annemarie Atapattu, Our Work Matters. Catholic Church employers and employees in Australia. Pastoral Research Office, Australian Catholic Bishops Conference, 2017; Trudy Dantis & Robert Dixon, Building stronger parishes: project report, Pastoral Research Office, Australian Episcopal Conference, May 2015; Stephen Reid, Lay Pastoral Ministry, Pointers, Volume 25 No. 4, December 2015, 8-10, Christian Research Association; Robert Dixon, Catholic Church employers and employees in Australia, Pointers, Volume 28, No 1, March 2018; Christian Research Association, 9-11, National Church Life Survey reports; Lutheran Church of Australia under headings of professional pastoral supervision, review of ministry, vocational development review, and many others.
13. Royal Commission.

# Chapter 8
# Leading Through Moral Discernment

Previously we argued that leadership, while crucial to the success of institutions and groups, is a complex and sometimes contradictory process, often due to the purpose and motivations of the leaders. Some differences in approach were identified when leadership has been equated with management and administration. While critical elements within many leadership roles require administration and management, they do not constitute leadership. We have proposed that, for the purposes of influencing institutions or groups with a community service foundation and mission (such as hospitals, schools and parishes), it is helpful to view leadership as a transrelational process. Using literature and research from the last 20 years, we have found traditional models of leadership fall short in their failure to help leaders understand the moral and ethical purpose of their roles. We then drew attention to new models including 'transforming' leadership[1], 'broad directional vision' for leadership[2], 'values based' leadership[3], leadership as 'moral action'[4] and 'moral praxis'[5], and, importantly for a synodal approach, 'transrelational' leadership[6]. We emphasised how this paradigm shift focuses leadership on discernment for moral outcomes.

We believe the adoption of a moral lens is needed to focus on appropriate responses to the values and moral needs of leaders' institutional followers. As a result of competing value pressures, there is a natural tension in the lives of leaders in leading and improving the institutional culture they lead.

For example, education is experiencing tension between leading for improved student performance and authentic learning objectives. (The first is measured by high stakes testing with the educational purpose of academic success. The second focuses on character development and views the purpose of education as being the transformation of the learner into a fuller, richer and more complete human being. Similarly, competition and tension sometimes exist between efficiency measurements of patient care using health and patient outcomes, and the same service measured by administrators using financial costs of service in hospitals and nursing homes. The capability of leaders to discern, articulate and prioritise valued outcomes has been the focus of the work of Burford & Pettit. Their research identified the existence of multiple contexts that act to influence a leader's capacity for and conduct of discernment as a precursor to moral decision making and action. To frame these competing purposes and aid discernment for decision making, they developed the Values and Purposes Taxonomy.[7]

## Values and Purposes Taxonomy

Earlier research reported that leaders in service organisations experience moral and ethical tensions when discerning and balancing the demands of competing stakeholders.[8] That study found that leaders require frames of reference that can assist them to lead in situations of uncertainty, ambiguity and seeming contradictions or paradox. The challenges facing leaders in this Service Organisations Leadership Research (SOLR) project were complex and multidimensional, with many challenges presenting themselves as tensions where value choices were often between right-right, as well as the more straightforward right-or-wrong alternatives. Finding optimal resolutions to such tension demanded mindsets and approaches requiring discernment of the competing value elements and purposes within the dilemma.

Burford and Pettit posited that moral decision making could be facilitated by a process of discernment in such dilemmas and tensions and developed a model with three dimensions and six contexts. This model was designed to provide a classification of the values position for moral discernment.[9] Hopefully, the model can aid understanding of the interaction between the different contexts and subsequent tensions in forming one's values position. The dimensions and the contexts requiring discernment are: The Interior (Moral and Personal Contexts), The Functional (Professional and Organisational Contexts) and The Environmental (Public and Cultural Contexts). The six contexts have overlapping yet differing origins and are interrelated in a sometimes complimentary but often conflicting manner. The values and purposes associated with these six contexts interact naturally and are experienced by leaders at differing levels and strengths as they seek direction through the process of moral discernment for decision making. The model is illustrated in Diagram 8.1.

The dashed lines between the intersecting contexts indicate the fluid nature of the interactions between each context, with no one context being exclusive from the influence of others. Each will be examined in turn to indicate its influence on discernment as a basis for subsequent leadership action.

### Dimension 1: Interior

The first two contexts rest in the interior and deeply personal values of leaders, their beliefs, character and needs. At the heart of this dimension rests the moral context.

### *Moral Context*

This first element is aligned with 'moral purpose' and incorporates the dynamic living out of character, values, ethical beliefs and commitments of the leader. Moral purpose focuses on what we believe is our foundational contribution to society, our responsibility for the lives of others and the commitment to act in ways that are consistent with our moral reasoning about the right, true, good and praiseworthy in our life. This is congruent with the centre of Starratt's framework of moral responsibility where leadership is seen to reside in the core of the leader as a human being rather than in observed behaviours and measured outcomes.[10]

The importance of the moral purpose and values of the leader was seen as a key element in building strong cultures around the core mission of the organisation. Other writers support this position, stressing the importance of leaders utilising and developing their sense of moral purpose so as to give purpose to others a consistent element in re-forming cultures and building capacity for change in groups or institutions.[11] Tom Sergiovanni described this position as 'the struggle to do the right thing according to a sense of values and what it means to be a human being'.[12] In the context of education, Frick describes this as the way 'moral considerations should be grounded in the *prima facie* principle: serve the best interests of the student'[13], while in hospitals and health care the foundational principle is 'do no harm'. Others identify a broader moral principle effecting the overall wellbeing and 'best interest' of members.[14] The difficulty with this broad 'best interest' principle is the complexity of identifying a priority between interests and the critical measurement of what is the 'best' of competing

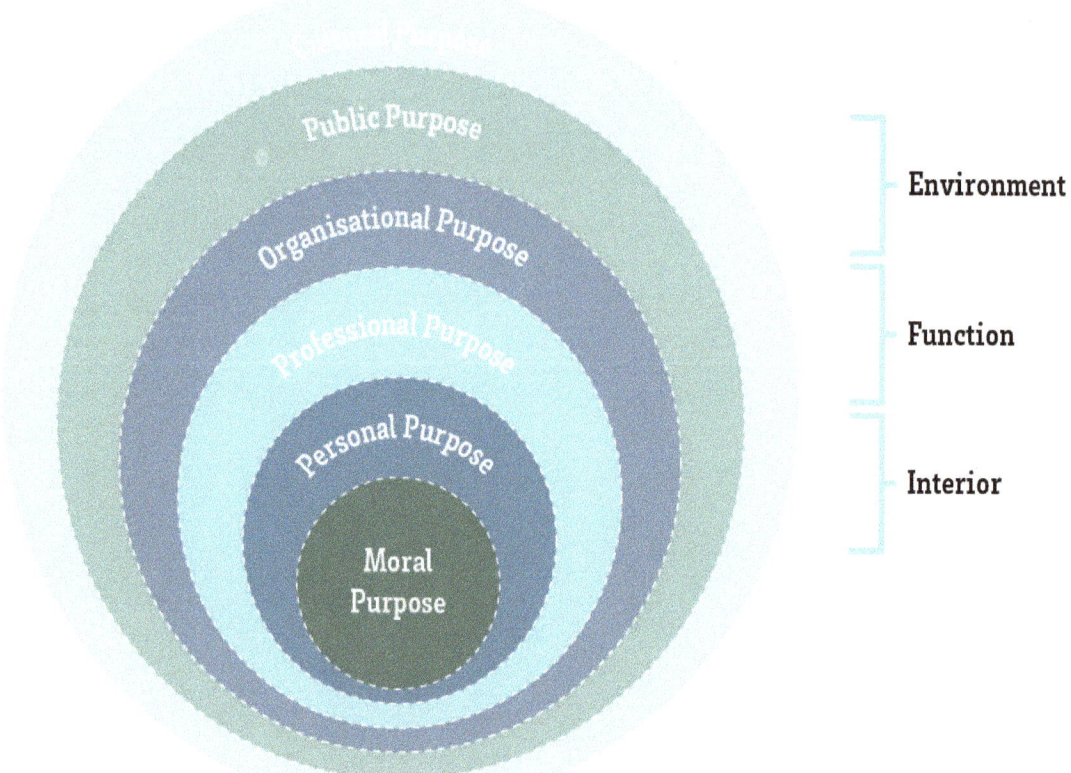

Diagram 8.1. Values and purposes taxonomy from Burford & Pettit

alternatives. Within the Church, these guiding principles are founded in the mission of Jesus Christ. This challenge of being true to moral purpose asks each diocese, school, parish, hospital or community group to be clear and explicit about its mission's core principles and to attempt to build consensus with all stakeholders around these principles.[15]

An Australian project on school improvement, titled Innovative Designs for Enhancing Achievements in Schools (IDEAS), found a shared sense of purpose, grounded in a shared commitment to explicit values, as being crucial to cultural improvement.[16] In other words, it is not sufficient to have a broad aspiration for change. There needs to be clarity and detail in the way the purpose is understood – and particularly in the values that underpin the change. Research has found that clear and explicit dialogue between stakeholders about the values at the core of change is related to the emergence of a sense of shared purpose.[17] The message here is that we need to engage in dialogue about our core purpose with those who share our profession or ministry so as to reinforce the reason for being together.

A question for leaders to ask themselves is: 'What should I do if I am to make a genuine difference in the lives of my people?' Clearly a leader who contributes to practices that are not authentic to the purpose and values of their institution and people, is probably engaging in behaviour which is morally wrong.[18] That such a self-evident fact about the abuse of the young escaped the attention of so many in institutions, including clergy and Church leaders, was one of the most confronting and challenging realisations to emerge from the findings of the Royal Commission. One's beliefs are not sufficient to effectively turn purpose into action. A consideration of the deeply personal aspects affecting one's motivations and behaviours is needed to build moral purpose. In this way the moral context of the synodal leader in the Church will be experienced by a spirituality of discipleship, and through dialogue, discernment, subsidiarity, consensus, reciprocal listening, walking together, co-responsibility and service.

### Personal Context

The second interior discernment element refers to the capacity of individuals to understand their reasons for acting. This 'personal context' considers links between one's beliefs and action and shows how attitudes can affect behaviour and practices. This context stresses the importance of the values and beliefs that form self-concept and identity, and which guide moral consciousness, sensitivity and actions in individuals.[19] Such reflective processes are seen as foundational to leaders 'living out ethical beliefs and commitments'.[20]

In this context the leader builds on moral purpose and carries over this commitment into the context of their personal needs. The moral and personal purpose also needs to be situated in the reality of having the power and ability (potency) to have a 'sense of their own capacity to make a difference in pursuing this purpose, and ultimately act courageously in its pursuit'[21]. This requires a clear understanding of who we are, what we value and believe, and what such commitment looks like in action. Activity 3.3 on credo development challenges us to create such an alignment of nominated core values.

Branson and Duignan have both stressed the importance not only of addressing a moral issue cognitively, but also of owning the outcome self-reflectively, rather than simply reacting to a situation.[22] Through this reflective interrogation of self, leaders rise above self-interest to act morally, or at least have a better understanding as to why they have failed to act morally. This insight might be as old as Socrates who named 'knowing oneself' as the beginning of wisdom, but history shows leaders need constant reminders about it. Such moral leadership 'is centrally concerned with ethics and morality and with deciding what is significant, what is right and what is worthwhile.'[23]

Identifying the influence of our upbringing, education, personal relationships and culture can give insight and power to understanding our values, purpose and faith. Discerning the strength and potency of personally held values can also give insights into what we view as our 'virtuous self'. Virtues need not be rational or logical, but can be viewed as a preferred way of being that points us towards our beliefs about what we ought to be or do in the face of dilemmas and tensions. For example, devotion to a vocation according to a congregation's founding charism can give differing value priorities and sometime lead to tensions within the same faith orientation. Franciscans live out their role according to the virtues professed by St. Francis, while Sisters of St Joseph uphold the virtues of St. Mary MacKillop. Both share the values and beliefs of a common Catholic faith but celebrate differing and preferred elements of that faith. Understanding what we see as our virtues and how we live them out in relationships is core to understanding the interior life that gives meaning to our leadership.

### Dimension 2: Function

The next dimension of function encompasses the leader's discernment of their role or ministry in an institution or group ('professional context'), as well as the context of the institution in which they operate ('organisational context').

### Professional Context

The 'professional context' includes the norms and codes of conduct relating to a leader's profession or ministry whereby they operate within a code of behaviour in the performance of their role. Here, core values and beliefs about the significance of the contribution of the profession or ministry to society are bound up in professional ethics or standards; and it is these values and beliefs that define what is the 'right thing to do' within that profession[24]. This requires a clear understanding of their function and role, its core function, and boundaries. The concept also involves a leader's understanding of how they can influence outcomes.

In education, for example, the professional context is expressed in constructs such as pedagogy, authentic learning, staff relations, confidentiality and privacy of stakeholders, collegiality and role performance. In Australia, the professional context for school leaders has been defined in the Australian Professional Standard for Principals which describes 'excellence in school leadership' as consisting of three leadership requirements: 1) vision and values; 2) knowledge and understanding; and 3) personal qualities and social and interpersonal skills. These leadership requirements work in tandem with five professional practices: i) leading teaching and learning; ii) developing self and others; iii) leading improvement, innovation and change; iv) leading the management of the school; and v) engaging and working with the community to form the leadership requirements and professional practices for school leaders.[25] In schools, these requirements and practices that define the professional standards are used to judge performance in the role; in practice, competing purposes and tensions complicate perceptions and actions.

Within positions of leadership in the Church, including the ordained, there are usually clear expectations of what a role means, even if formal standards have not yet been developed; here too, these professional understandings are impacted, both consciously and unconsciously, by issues of values, personality, education, training, traditions and culture, especially the culture of clericalism. Much debate about change in the Catholic Church today is driven by understandings related to the expectations and beliefs that have been formed about the authority of priests and bishops in the Church. Current discussion and contests between clerical and synodal culture and power are infused with meaning about theological beliefs, divergent ecclesiologies, the history and importance of ecclesial authority, and the country in which it is operating. Tensions and dilemmas often reside in the differing expectations and demands of others, usually associated with their understanding and expectations of the role of the profession. Understanding this force of compliance towards the norms of professions can give insights into the contesting that sometimes occurs, particularly when demands of others contest the interior values of the leader. The Plenary Council faces these questions about change, especially those related to the role of women, the inadequacies of the response of Church leaders to the abuse of children by congregations and clergy, and transparent and accountable governance.

Ambiguity and variability about how the roles of Church members are lived out and justified has led to pushback by

Church communities, coupled with accusations of irrelevance of positions and processes.[26]

### Organisational Context

This context encompasses what an institution values and celebrates, and how this influences the way leadership, management, resourcing and relationships are conducted, both within the entity itself and with external bodies. The culture of the organisation or 'how we do things around here' is at the heart of this context.

*In a large suburban parish, the parish priest is working to implement a vision that will bring all ministries together, within a culture of a shared understanding of their mission. At the same time, he is arranging to recruit key staff for the parish office, oversee their orientation, attend to risk management and courses in cyber security, attend diocesan meetings, preside at Masses for the opening of the school year, attend to the normal calendar of the Church. The purposes are many, varied and often competing with the culture that the parish priest is trying to build. It will require discernment, understanding and determination at the grass roots level if renewal is to take place in this organisation called Church.*

The meaning and purpose of Church structures and processes are rooted in scriptures, teachings and history of the Church, but the challenges facing Church renewal will probably rest in how these beliefs and attitudes are valued and shared by varying populations of the faithful. In many cases, values at the interior level will unite Church members at all levels given the commonality of beliefs from education, family backgrounds and faith experiences, but understandings and vested positions about clerical authority, dogma and ecclesial imperatives can vary dramatically and loom as areas of tension and conflict between the faithful in renewal endeavours. To change the culture of Church ministries away from clericalism towards greater accountability, transparency, co-responsible governance and synodality needs to be a deliberate process, as noted in a recent Catholic Leadership Summit in the USA.[27] Cultures move slowly and unevenly, as observers of the implementation of the vision of Vatican II can attest.

Leaders are being faced with increasing pressure to make conscious adaptations to their practices, often resulting in 'intrapersonal moral discord', dilemmas, and tensions about the 'why' of change initiatives. Further, the concept of moral purpose that is 'socially just' has become a key element in re-forming cultures and building capacity for renewal.

Together, the professional and organisational contexts, describe the interplay between the leader and others' attitudes and perceptions of the role in concert with organisational dimensions that frame the system's culture. In conjunction with the interior dimension the stage is now set to consider the third dimension of the wider societal and cultural setting that affects the leader's capacity for moral discernment described as the environment.

### Dimension 3: Environment

This dimension relates to the external parts of a leader's influence. While not having direct control over these, the leader must operate within these wider societal and cultural influences that are often related to tensions surrounding accountability, compliance and responsibility due to external sources of control, which can often be at odds with the interior and functional dimensions.

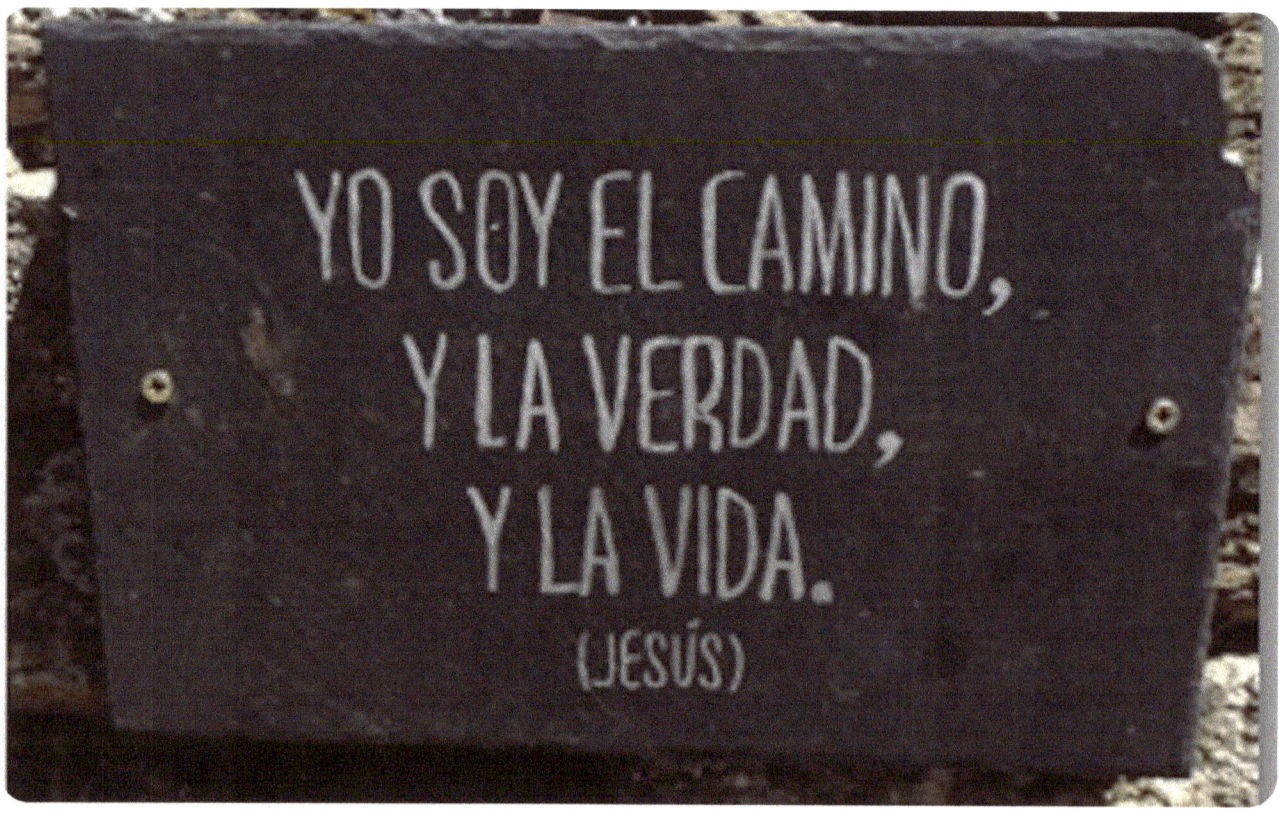

## Public Content

Organisations exist within an internal and external jurisdictional setting and sets of accountability frameworks that impact on leaders' actions. Government and system requirements and accountabilities, particularly when tied to funding and resourcing, influence the exercise of leadership, as does the work of pressure groups which may be at variance with the mission of the institution and the leader.

Again, taking education as an example, school leaders are accountable for leading change, improving learning and reporting performance. Research suggests that this has created a tension between being accountable for these learning processes through measurement and reporting of student performance on the one hand, and the moral obligation to use information on student achievement to effect improvement in student outcomes on the other.[28] These public accountabilities when exercised by independent religious groups, such as dioceses and parishes, can be the source of tension for a Church accustomed to internal authority and accountability.

One example of this tension was the introduction and acceptance of the A-E assessment policy mandated for Australian schools. The fact that many educators did not appreciate, or respect the educational philosophy of the policy, yet had to accept the obligation of accepting Government policy as part of funding agreements, had implications for the independence and accountability of the religious system to the funding government. As Susan Pascoe observes:

> This meant that the administrative and support role of Catholic Education Offices for schools went beyond professional support, religious education and canonical requirements to a de facto compliance enforcement role. It is not an option to take the funding and ignore the conditions, no matter how contentious or trivial. These significant contractual requirements need to be better understood.[29]

This clear tension in public accountability has been the source of ongoing challenges for health, educational and service groups in the Church, although it has been more pronounced in education as the Catholic education leaders in diocesan systems are directly responsible to Bishops, which isn't as pronounced in health and social services. Funding by the Federal and State Government of Catholic education in Australia is regulated and Church schools and/or systems must not only account for the use of government funds but must ensure there is no use of these funds by other Church services. Importantly in the public arena, accountability for decisions can have a large influence on the leader's willingness and ability to move from moral purpose to moral action in such conflicting circumstances.[30] In 2020, the Australian Federal Government announced new policies to 'make non-government systems, which are given lump sum funding payments, more accountable for the way taxpayer funding is moved around to different schools ... amid ongoing sensitivity over the way Catholic authorities distribute their resources'.[31]

It is concerning to see that the Government has to raise moral concerns about the willingness of Catholic authorities to show transparency and accountability in the use of public funds. This stresses the need for the Church to show clear moral and ethical accountability in its leadership. It is our position that it is the Church and its leaders who should be the guardians of such ethical expectations regarding our public processes, not the reverse.

## Cultural Context

The final element is the 'cultural context' which involves understanding the broad social and cultural and political contexts in which the institution operates. Differences in values, beliefs and practices associated with cultural variations of different nations that make up the Church have been identified as existing not just between Northern and Southern Hemispheres but between developing and first world countries. The construct we have proposed of culture is based on its importance to leadership, the achievement of mission, and the perceived authenticity of how the institution operates in relation to the Church. Here we are referring to the influence of broad cultural values and purposes of peoples and nations. The varying characteristics of states, regions, and even interest and belief groups, are expressed at this level.

Recently, a serving General of the Australian special services, when speaking to Special Air Services (SAS) about accusations of war crimes and atrocities by troops from these forces in Afghanistan, pointed to their distinguished history but claimed the strength of the culture of the SAS had been contaminated by 'poor leadership ... In fact it is poor moral leadership'.[32] Strong service cultures like that experienced in the military, police, custodial and community services, can become a danger to themselves, as suggested in this example, due to a misplaced sense of loyalty and group cohesion. This creates additional moral leadership demands to ensure the culture's values stay on mission.

National and cultural differences in the Church have also created tensions with issues such as married clergy, (viewed as crucial to the survival of the South American Church), the Australian cultural value of egalitarianism, and the first world realisation and demand for equality of the sexes. It is appropriate that the Church would lead in issues of accountability and equity, such as financial transparency and moral responsibility for sexually offending clergy. The future of the universal Church will be influenced by how this challenge is faced.

Ultimately, the cultural authenticity of the Church will rest in communities' expectations of the purpose of their faith and the Church's capacity to match that purpose. The Plenary Council faces growing evidence that the culture of the young, multi-cultural and secular orientated Australian communities has shifted in relation to values and beliefs about religion and the Church. These issues have been further complicated by the history of child abuse in the Church, its attitude to the role of women in ministries, the post-modernist distrust of all organisations, and a general questioning of the relevance of faith to the life of young twenty-first century Australians. These and other cultural challenges are not new, but they are now irrepressible and require discernment and understanding by the Church if it is to be relevant to Australia's future.

## Conclusion

We suggest that Values and Purpose Taxonomy can provide important insights into the many, often-competing, contexts that leaders experience in moral decision-making. These contexts involve the leader's interior values and beliefs, the functional view of their role within an institution, the multidimensional aspects of the institution itself, as well as the wider socio-cultural influences affecting their leadership. All these influences will impact on forming, and informing, the leaders' processes of moral discernment, decision making and action, which we view as the purpose of leadership.

## Activity 8.1: Ethics in leadership

Consider a situation you have experienced in the last year as a leader or a member of a team. Reflect on what happened in the situation. Then ask the following questions following the process taken from the Ethical Decision-Making Model of Stefkovich and Shapiro according to the ethics of justice, care, critique or the profession.

**Justice:**

- Is there a law, right, or policy that would be appropriate for resolving a particular ethical dilemma?
- Why is this law, right or policy the correct one for this particular case?
- How should the law, right or policy be implemented?

**Critique:**

- Who makes the laws, rules or policies?
- Who benefits from these laws, rules or policies?
- Who has the power?
- Who are the silenced voices?

**Care:**

- Who will benefit from what I decide?
- Who will be hurt by my actions?
- What are the long-term effects of a decision I make today?
- If I am helped by someone now, what should I do in the future about giving back to this individual or to society in general?

**Profession:**

- What is in the best interests of stakeholders?
- What are the personal and professional behavioural codes that should be considered?
- What professional organisations' codes of ethics should be considered?
- What does the local community think about this issue?
- What is the appropriate way for a professional to act in this particular situation, based on the standards of the profession?

## Activity 8.2: Interior reflection

Below is piece of prose by the great American philosopher and poet Walt Whitman. Read it and consider what he is saying to us about understanding the moral and personal purposes in our lives. Read privately, reflect and record your responses. Share, if comfortable, with a friend or colleague:

> This is what you shall do: love the earth and sun and the animals, despise riches, give alms to everyone that asks, stand up for the stupid and crazy, devote your income and labour to others, hate tyrants, argue not concerning God, have patience and indulgence towards the people, take off your hat to nothing known or unknown or to any person or number of person, go freely with powerful undereducated persons and with the young and with the mothers of families.
>
> Read these leaves in the open air every season of every year of your life, re-examine all you have been told at school or Church or in any book, dismiss whatever insults your own soul, and your very flesh shall be a great poem and have the richest fluency not only in its words but in the silent lines of its lips and face and between the lashes of your eyes and in every motion and joint of your body ...

– **Walt Whitman, Preface, *Leaves of Grass*, 1855**

## Activity 8.3: Power in leadership

Why should a person do what their leader asks them to do? What provides the leader with the power to get others to complete desired outcomes? What elements of leadership seem to enhance or hinder your sense of ownership and fulfilment in your role in the Church, school, hospital or health or welfare organisation?

We are told some traditional perceived sources of power – such as position, coercion or knowledge – are no longer accepted unquestioningly.

- How does this assertion match your experience of leadership in your school, parish, council, board, hospital or health care institution?
- Does the Taxonomy of Values and Purposes Model improve your motivation?
- Discuss your reaction with other members of your staff, team, committee or board.
- How has this exercise helped you understand the nature of leadership where you serve?

## Endnotes

1. R. M. Burns
2. M. Fullan, Large-scale reform comes of age, *Journal of Educational Change*, 10, 2009, pp. 101-103; Starratt, 2012, p. 109.
3. P. T. Begley, Values and leadership: Theory development, new research, and an agenda for the future, *Alberta Journal of Educational Research*, 46:3, 2000, pp. 233-249.
4. T. Sergiovanni, The virtues of leadership, in *The Educational Forum*, 69:2, 2005, pp. 112-123.
5. W. Frick, Principals' Value-informed decision making, intrapersonal moral discord, and pathways to resolution: the complexities of moral leadership praxis., *Journal of Educational Administration*, 47:1, 2009, pp. 50-74.
6. Branson et al., 2019
7. C. Burford & P. Pettit, A conceptual model for linking values, discernment and outcome perception, *Values and Ethics in Educational Administration*, 13:2, 2018, p. 1-9.
8. P. Duigan & C. Burford, *SOLR project: Contemporary challenges and implications for leaders in frontline human service organisations*, ACU National, Sydney, 2003.
9. Burford & Pettit, 2018.
10. R. Starratt in S. Doscher & A. Nomore, The moral agency of the educational leader in times of national crisis and conflict, *Journal of School Leadership*, 18:1, 2008, pp. 8-31.
11. B. Levin & M. Fullan, 2008. Learning about system renewal, *Educational Management Administration Leadership*, 36:2, 2008, p. 294.
12. T. Sergiovanni, 2005, p. 11.
13. W. Frick, p. 53.
14. J. A. Stefkovich & P. T. Begley, *Ethical school leadership: Defining the best interests of students*, Educational Management Administration & Leadership, 35:2, 2007, pp. 205-224.
15. See K. Rowe, Assessment, league tables and school effectiveness: Consider the issues and 'let's get real'!, Journal of Educational Enquiry, 1:1, 2000, pp.73-98; R. Starratt, Leading a community of learners: Learning to be moral by engaging the morality of learning, *Educational Management Administration Leadership*, 35:2, 2007, pp. 165-183.
16. D. Andrews, School revitalisation the IDEAS way, *ACEL Monograph*, 34, 2004.
17. M. Bezzina & C. Burford, 2010 Leaders transforming learning and learners: An Australian innovation in leadership, learning and moral purpose., in A. Normore (ed.), *Global perspectives on educational leadership reform: The development and preparation of leaders of learning and learners of leadership*, Emerald Group, Bingley UK, pp. 265-285.
18. Starratt, 2004.
19. See P. Begley & J. Stefkovich, Integrating values and ethics into post-secondary teaching for leadership development: principals, concepts and strategies, *Journal of Educational Administration*, 45:4, 2007, pp. 398-41; see especially the Model of Self in C. Branson, (2014) The power of personal values, in C. Branson & S. Gross (eds), *Handbook of Ethical Educational Leadership*, Routledge, New York, 2014, pp. 195-209; Burford & Pettit, 2011; D. Goleman; N. Tuana, Conceptualizing moral literacy, *Journal of Educational Administration*, 45:4, 2007, p. 364-378.
20. Starratt, 2004, p. 5.
21. Bezzina & Tuana, 2012 p. 13.
22. C. Branson, 2009; P. Duignan, 2007.
23. Duignan, 2007, p. 34.
24. W. C. Frick & J. F. Covaleskie, Preparation of integrity, in Branson & Gross, 2014, pp. 386-404.
25. Australian Institute for Teaching and School Leadership (AITSL), *Australian professional standards for principals*. 2011, retrieved from www.aitsl.edu.au.
26. GBOM, pp. 42-76.
27. Reported in Pascoe, 2019, p. 4.
28. J. Hattie, What is the nature of evidence that makes a difference to learning?, Paper presented at the *Using Data to Support Learning Research* Conference, Melbourne, 2005.
29. Pascoe, 2019, p..10.
30. See K.K. Abowitz, *Publics for public schools: Legitimacy, democracy, and leadership*, Paradigm Publishers, Boulder, 2013.
31. Fergus Hunter, Catholic school systems to face more funding transparency, *Sydney Morning Herald*, 6th July, 2020, https://www.smh.com.au/politics/federal/catholic-school-systems-to-face-more-funding-transparency-20200706-p559en.html
32. N. McKenzie & C. Masters, Special forces chief acknowledges war crimes, blames 'poor moral leadership, *Sydney Morning Herald*, 28 June, 2020, https://www.smh.com.au/national/special-forces-chief-acknowledges-war-crimes-blames-poor-moral-leadership-20200628-p556z6.html

# Chapter 9

# Moral Decision-making

Not only must a leader know what is right: they are required to act on such discernments to give their actions moral meaning and direction. As one scholar explained, 'a complete theory of moral agency must link moral knowledge and reasoning to moral conduct'.[1] This chapter will link the three dimensions of the Values Taxonomy to a Model for Moral Decision-Making. It will also address moral agency and moral potency through a Strategy for Moral Decision-Making[2]. This strategy we offer as a discernment process which incorporates questions about moral purpose, desired outcomes and the capacity or agency to implement moral decisions.

## A moral decision-making model

The extension from discernment to action described here is also captured in literature. A 'Four Component Model' explains the role of moral/ethical dispositions in decision-making. This process moves from 'moral sensitivity' in interpreting a particular situation, through 'moral judgment' (or the ability to judge actions as morally right or wrong), to 'moral motivation' (where moral values are prioritised), then to 'moral character' (where the consequences for all affected by the decision, including the decision maker, are considered).[3] An insight to this process of discernment is as follows: 'If an individual recognises the various factors of an ethical situation (sensitivity), makes a sound ethical decision (judgment), and places moral values over one's personal values (motivation), then that individual is prepared to execute a moral action (character).'[4]

In exploring this link between beliefs and action, another model of moral literacy extends the earlier positions to include ethics sensitivity, ethical reasoning skills and moral imagination, and providing an ethical framework to effect moral agency, whereby we become 'ethical agents' who are able to 'assess what is held to be valuable in a context'.[5] Other writers speak of failure in agency due to a 'gap between moral purpose and moral performance',[6] 'ethical blindness',[7] and the absence of 'realised moral purpose'[8]. Michael Bezzina and Nancy Tuana noted that prior to acting with moral purpose and showing agency, leaders need a sense of the influence available to them to make a decision that will make a difference, their 'moral potency'. The major influences on their capacity to act will be 'their ownership of, and commitment to, moral purpose; their sense of hope; and the requisite courage to act'.[9]

As an example of such courage, we referred previously to an Australian Army General condemning the lack of moral leadership in the culture of the Australian Special Air Services as contributing to possible war crimes and atrocities in Afghanistan. In condemning the poor leadership, he pointed to whistle-blowers within these forces who reported on these events and referred to their actions as 'moral courage'[10] – the courage to go against a cultural force for moral reasons. The same can also be said of victims of sexual abuse who have spoken out and the many whistleblowers who have given witness to corruption, specifically in Australian banks, politics and police. The process of making a decision, having discerned the moral position of the value conflict, and then achieving a moral outcome through moral agency, is shown in Diagram 9.1 on the following page.

This process is built upon the premise of the user first forming (and informing) a values position (using the earlier taxonomy). This is a precursor to moral discernment which may then involve taking some action, or sometimes the decision not to act at all; a decision influenced by moral courage, agency and potency. Even though a leader may be 'morally literate' with a sensitivity that tunes and gives direction to their moral compass, a particular moral action will only be chosen if they feel they are capable of effecting influence and have the capacity to act – the condition we have described as moral potency.[11]

Moral potency becomes an influential element in determining how values and purpose concerns may influence action. Being context-bound, the potency of the decision can be influenced by the varying purposes, as outlined in the Taxonomy. This helps explain why leaders may not necessarily translate beliefs into action, despite knowing that it is in the best interests of followers to do so.[12] For example, let us consider contemporary broad societal issues, such as climate change, refugees and low-cost housing. These all are issues that have certain levels of universal appeal, but political and cultural forces act against many people's sense of being able to effect a resolution. This speaks to a lack of moral potency where political forces undermine individual citizens' potency. Similarly, the culture of clericalism may account for a sense of powerlessness and a perceived lack of potency experienced by clergy and congregations in the face of the challenges facing them in changing the Church's culture towards a more synodal model. The perception that we can't make a difference rests in this perceived lack of potency.

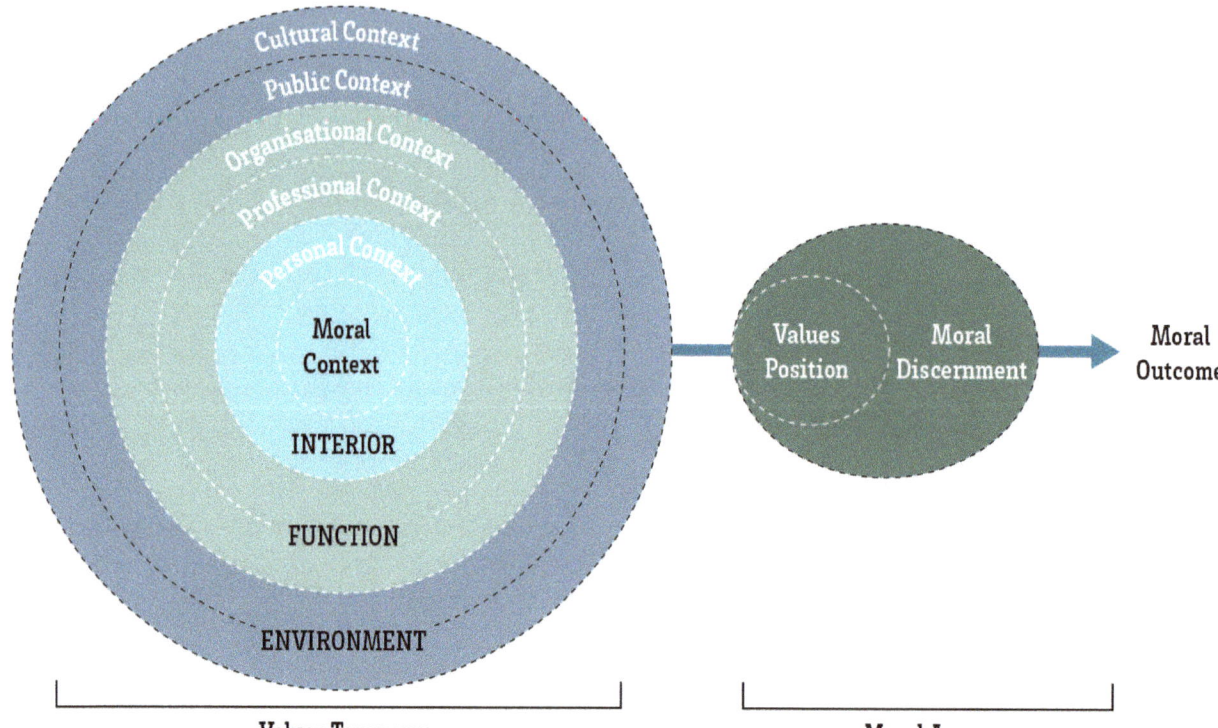

**Values Taxonomy** — **Moral Agency**

Diagram 9.1. Moral decision-making model

The complications relating to moral potency reinforce the importance of leaders being able to give an explicit, articulated and practical priority to values and purposes regarding outcomes for those they lead. Using the taxonomy can provide important insights into the sources of potential misunderstandings, tensions and inevitable conflict that leaders will experience in moral decision-making processes. The possibility of agency and the potential of potency should be outcomes of a leader's discernment achieved through using the model. Some situations where agency and potency of moral decision-making is required by those in governance or leadership within the Church, as identified by one researcher, might include:

- considerations of merging parishes (or alternatives) in the face of declining numbers and ageing clergy,
- management of a situation where a senior leader needs to be stood down or dismissed,
- introduction of legislation or regulation that appears to be in direct conflict with the Church's teaching and the ethos of a given ministry, such as Voluntary Assisted Dying, abortion, marriage equality
- balancing legal obligations that come with accepting Government funding against institutional values and conflicting expectations of a diocesan financial administrator,
- responding to the whole person when the response is not consistent with Church teaching, (e.g. with increasing possible intervention via medical technology, employing divorced, LGBTIQ+, safe injecting rooms),
- respecting each staff member's personal meaning system while requiring formation in the ethos of the particular ministry within the Church's mission, and

- Catholic or competent, selecting the best person for a role while balancing institutional expectations about religious practice/affiliation (e.g., teacher, researcher, social worker, principal, department head).[13]

The final decision to exercise agency will rest with the individual's moral courage and capacity, and their motivation and potency to act and to assist in this process. We now offer the following Strategy for Moral Decision-Making.

## Strategy for moral decision-making

This strategy asks overarching questions about the decision-making process. The strategy includes stressing the importance of identifying facts influencing the tension and motivations of participants, the generation and selecting of alternative actions, and discernment as to the moral and virtuous outcomes of the decision. The strategy incorporates 10 requisites as shown in Table 9.2.[14]

### Applying the strategy

The strategy for moral decision-making is designed to reflect the theoretical perspective of transrelational leadership. Branson et al[15] described this as a leadership praxis that moves others to a far more effective level of functioning by means of relationships. In this relational context the strategy requires the leader to consider the type of tension prompting the need for action; the facts surrounding the events leading to the identification of the tension; the motivations and capacity of participants that could help or hinder the quality of the decision; how the process should acknowledge the rights of those effected, and how to be a moral agent to ensure the success of the decision implementation.

We will now expand each of the ten requisites of the moral

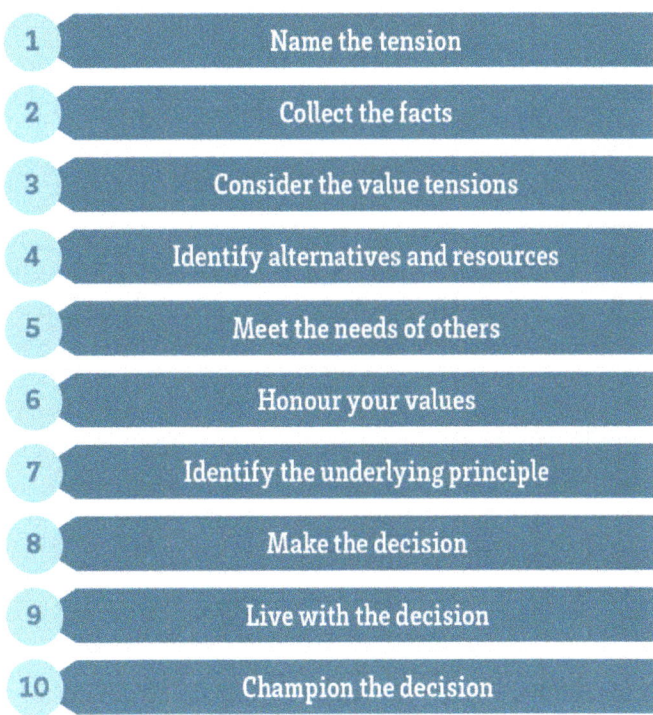

Table 9.1 Requisites of moral decision-making

decision-making strategy that attempt to resolve dilemmas in institutions.

### Name the tension

The first step in the strategy asks the leader to pose questions about the concern that has been identified as requiring action. Is there a problem and/or tension? If so, is it restricted to themself or does it involve others?

Once the leader is certain there is a problem and who is involved, they should attempt to identify if it has a professional, institutional, or cultural element that needs to be considered. Is it a personal dispute or does it have specific professional, managerial, governance, ecclesial, theological or cultural origins? Does it have a moral or ethical component? Is it a tension within the leader themself? (For example, does it raise issues of rights, justice, the good of the community, professional standards, duty?) The dimensions and contexts of the Values and Purpose Taxonomy can be helpful here in locating the origins of the tension.

### Collect the facts

This step involves identifying and describing the facts associated with the tension. This may require seeking evidence from others so as to gain a balanced and comprehensive picture about the circumstances of the problem. A focus on the stakes and interests of players and contributing factors, such as policy, authority, politics or culture, may give insights into underlying bias or ideology. Stake and motivations could be assisted by answering the question: What is at risk for the people or groups involved and how strongly are the positions held that are in dispute? Using the Values and Purposes Taxonomy try to identify the location of the problem's dimensions and contexts according to your factual analysis, the core of the tension and the motivations of the participants. To assist with this analysis, motivations can be broadly categorised to fall under descriptions such as those concerned with i) the self, involving personal preference, habit and comfort; ii) desired outcomes, focusing on the avoidance of the undesirable and grounded in consequences; iii) the opinion of others, rational values grounded in consensus (usually through consultation or expert opinion), and iv) ethical and moral purpose.

The 2020 protests in Australia about black deaths in custody were ignited initially by the Black Lives Matter protests and riots in America after the death of an African American, George Floyd, at the hands of police in Minnesota. This occurred at the same time as critical health restrictions were being enforced due to the Covid-19 pandemic and concerns regarding social distancing. The decision to march and protest or observe the State and Federal government pleas to stay away, constituted just such an ethical and moral problem – two goods involving different values. Racial injustice and protecting the common good and health of the community stood face to face. Motivations rested at all of the four levels identified above and leaders struggled to find the best solution. The tension was real and deeply felt; many spoke to the conflict and some passed judgement publicly, driven by the interests of their motivations, ideology, politics, culture or life story. Having facts helps, but that will not remove the influence of value tensions.

### Consider the value tensions

Another task is to consider the consequences of giving priority to one context, value or purpose at the expense of another or others. What will impact on the other competing values and purposes? Is a decision necessary at a dichotomous level? That is, is it necessarily an either/or decision between two or several contexts? Or could it be a both/and solution incorporating elements of more than one context?

In the example of the Black Deaths in Custody marches and the threat to the health of the community, the value tensions of the common good reflected in the biosecurity of the population conflicted with the need to express rights regarding longstanding injustice in American and Australian societies. The majority of political leaders opted for the political clarity of the health of the common good position while speaking to the recognition of the injustice, but some condemned protesters as thoughtless and irresponsible.

Many Catholics underwent similar value tensions during the Royal Commission. Their Church and everything they cherished and loved about their faith was being challenged and they were being forced to confront the truth of the sexual abuse. The fact that the Church leadership in Australia failed in identifying the tensions of the people they lead was attested to by Archbishop Coleridge, Chair of the Australian Catholic Bishops Conference.[16] Did the Bishops ask the 'value questions' when they moved offending priests to other unsuspecting parishes, or when they refused to reveal these criminal behaviours to the legal authorities? One hopes the answer is 'No,' as the alternative is a horrible reality to accept. On the other hand, if they were considering conflicting values (such as loyalty as opposed to justice), their decision-making would appear to have been faulty at best.

### Identify alternatives and resources

The coverage of the moral decision-making model highlights the need for discernment of moral rightness of decisions and the need to decide between sometimes competing but often complementary alternatives.

In these situations, having identified that there is a problem, ascertained the facts and what critical values are in contest, we need to identify alternative actions or solutions. At this stage, leaders can reflect on the availability of people and resources to assist in developing alternative solutions. Having identified people with expertise in the area of concern, both internally or externally, and material resources (such as publications, media, reports or exemplars of practice) the leader should next utilise these relevant and expert resources to generate alternative options and positions. These alternative actions that can be used as the basis for the collaborative stage, where all persons who will be affected are invited into the process. By utilising expert resources early in the process, the leader can enhance the quality of the final decision. Stakeholders will usually hold vested interests and sometimes loyalty to political positions that can detract from the quality of the decision. By involving stakeholders at the collaboration and decision acceptance stage, they can minimise political influencing, thus maximising ownership of the decision. Acknowledgement and commitment to the justice and equity of the decision-making and acceptance process will usually be a significant contribution to its success.

It is useful to pose the following questions. What individuals and/or groups have a right to be involved? How should such involvement be negotiated? These are important elements in the success of the process. Earlier we described how the construct of subsidiarity proclaimed by Pope Leo XIII in 1891 directed that those affected by a decision have a moral right to be involved in such decisions. As an institution that has evolved through the association of members drawn together by common values and beliefs, the Church could be expected to demonstrate the granting of the rights of subsidiarity to its own members in decisions affecting their spiritual and religious lives. The issue would appear not to be 'if' leaders in the Church should be involving concerned others in decision-making, but rather 'how' to identify who is affected and 'how' best to involve them in the process.

### Meet the needs of others

Which of the alternative decisions will best meet the needs of the significant other/s involved in the tension? As identified earlier, the decision that stands the best chance of meeting needs is that which is owned. And ownership is best achieved by how the significant participants and consumers view the decision-making process. Not only must the process be transparent, it must be assessable, accountable and available to members. If those leading the process of making the decision are trusted and the process promotes equity, fairness, collegiality, empowerment and respect, then those affected by the decision will accept it, even if they have not been directly involved. The absence of one principle may not hurt, but the perception that these characteristics are not valued by the leader will probably doom the acceptance of the decision and the success of any further invitation to share. Questions to help discern the needs of others and create valuable alternatives could include: What action or decision would maximise benefits for all stakeholders? What action or decision would best respect the individual rights of the participants and those affected? Are the desired 'ends' or outcomes of the leader interfering with the 'means' of reaching a decision?

Parish Councils that are enthusiastically endorsed by their parish leader in matters of finance and resources but resisted on issues related to faith, celebration, pastoral ministry or general responsibility for governance, will usually become distinguished by rapid turnover of members and a lack of ownership of responsibilities. Meeting the needs of others can be difficult but if the perceived primary purpose of leadership is the consistent meeting of the leaders' needs, all efforts for change will fail.[17] Synodal leaders serve others' needs first.

### Honour your values

Earlier we indicated that virtues were the preferred values and beliefs about what we believe is essential to our sense of self.

'Self' was also identified in the moral and personal context of the Taxonomy of Values and Purpose. The interior life of the leader is where the important battles about the rightness and/or wrongness of decisions or actions are usually fought out, but it is also where the self-image of who we are at our best resides. Recognising what our best looks like is an exercise in virtue recognition and is an essential part of a transrelational approach to leadership. Having the capacity and ability to honour what we value, and know what we see as virtuous for us, is vitally important for others to see if we are to lead morally for transformation.

Honouring value and virtue is sometimes a challenge for those new to leadership. New leaders can sometimes understate their own value positions, partly because of trying to be 'objective' and partly because they fail to grasp the significance of their own value position for those with whom they work. When confronted with an ethical dilemma whereby exists two equally difficult and unacceptable alternatives, how do we react? Do we avoid making a decision? Suspend moral consequences for utilitarian purposes? Fall back to self-interest? Or take a moral stance despite consequences? Finally, to ensure the honouring of our virtues in this process, we need to reflect on what persons of good judgment will think of the justifications for this decision. Which decision would you like to defend to the ones you love, trust and respect the most?

One example of such a circumstance occurred when pastoral care triumphed over law on national television in Australia in June 2003.

> On 23 June, newly elected Jesuit Provincial Mark Raper, faced with the knowledge of abuse by a Jesuit colleague, accepted the advice of lawyers and declined to appear on the National Broadcaster's 7.30 Report to discuss the allegations. However, as reported in the Sydney Morning Herald, the next day the Provincial wrote a letter of 'profound apology' to the victim; furthermore, he appeared on a subsequent 7.30 Report program where he said he had been accepting advice against his better judgement and to ignore that advice had been a 'moment of liberation'. It had been 'sheer folly', he said, to let the 'legal area' dominate the 'pastoral area' and this wholly unhappy episode would mean an end to the way in which the Society (of Jesus) followed legal advice. Asked by the program host, what would happen if the Church's assets came under threat because of his change in approach, Mark Raper replied, 'the assets are not as important as the people that we seek to serve'.[18]

### *Identify the underlying principle*

Having followed the process to discern the best alternative for the context and circumstance of the given tension or problem, a last reflection on the generics of the process and possible outcomes can add to our understanding of leading and using moral decision-making approaches. Having decided that a decision is important for the needs of our mission, and for the reinforcement and progression of our own moral character, we need to ask which decision would contribute to the morality of the overall process?

Asking ourselves which decision would make a good general rule for people confronting a similar leadership tension in the future can elevate the process and outcome by giving it a social and cultural benefit. Subjecting the decision to the 'general rule for others' analysis can give increased insights into the quality of a final decision. If we are ready to expose the process and decision to transparent evaluation by an autonomous public, we have probably reached a position that reflects our virtuous 'best' self, as well as the mission and needs of our institution. Hopefully this will be a decision that contributes to helping others in similar situations. Identifying principles at the heart of decisions can be confronting but beneficial to others in similar circumstances. Articulating the priority of a principle such as 'the common good', 'freedom of information,' 'social justice,' 'duty of care' or the many 'rights' identified in many constitutions and professional codes, can give both clarity and direction to future decision-makers. Not wanting to appear on the front page of some sensational daily tabloids, does not qualify, we suggest, as a principle of any worth.

### *Make the decision*

Earlier we discussed the virtue and authenticity of institutions committed to synodality, involving others in decisions as colleagues, fellow pilgrims and partners in the journey of faith. Often the insights and wisdom of others and the benefits of collegial discourse will give the decision-making process a moral foundation, but it may still leave the leader with final responsibility for the decision. Accountability, role restrictions, governance regulations and the law can demand that the ultimate decision must rest with the leader. In these

circumstances, following the recommended process, a leader should be able to make the decision with or without the aid of the stakeholders. However, how the decision is announced, explained and resourced is as crucial as the decision itself. Transparency of process, accuracy of information, relevance of communicating methods and openness to feedback, will all contribute to the successful acceptance of the decision.

> An example from education involved the leadership team in a diocesan system of schools choosing to involve all principals and senior staff (about 100 people) in the annual system planning. This was based on honouring the leader's values (Strategy #6).[19] The approach was not immediately welcomed: there were some divides between different areas of responsibility that found this merging-together of interests uncomfortable, even demeaning (Strategy #1). In time, with the creativity of many people, it was worked through. The process was sometimes quite messy. Again, together – and the whole process was heavily indebted to everyone who was involved – the 'College of Leaders' worked through the uncertainties and identified priorities for the next three-years, priorities that were reviewed and reflected in the budget (#4). It was not perfect. It was a recognition that those closest to the action in schools were a valuable resource in working through the tensions between competing values and demands (#4); and a process of discerning how to best meet the needs of the various school communities and their students (#5). Prayer and reflection were incorporated into the process. It was, in the terms of the strategy, an expression of identifying facts (Strategy #2), identifying value tensions (#3), identifying alternatives and resources for the decision-making process (#4) and discerning which decision would best meet the needs of those affected by the decision (#7). The final decision rested with the Executive (#8). It was also, in our terms, an expression of synodality and subsidiarity (# 9). Not only did the outcomes exceed what a small team of executives might dream up; the process of synodality generated energy, commitment and solidarity around shared values and hopes and the community of educational leaders was strengthened in their mission through the process.

### Live with the decision

Having made and delivered a decision, either as a member of a group or an individual, the leader should then address how best to make certain the decision can be lived with by stakeholders in such a way as to advance the purposes for which it was instituted. Through reviews and stakeholder colloquia, the decision should be exposed to the forces of institutional interrogation, reflection and evaluation. As Margaret Wheatley told us, 'We need leadership to understand that we are best controlled by concepts that invite participation, not policies and procedures that curtail our contribution. We all have to learn to support the workings of each other'.[20]

### Champion the decision

The final step is the need to become a champion for the decision. Stakeholders will take significance from the experience of how well a decision is enacted, resourced and celebrated. The leader can champion the decision by affirming the process used in reaching the decision, acclaim its benefits to the stakeholders, give support and resources to the implementers of the decision and celebrate their activities. This sometimes involves defending implementers against external threats and internal doubts and being available to allay fears about uncertainty and change.

The effects of an absence of championing is often seen in ministries where an issue is identified for a decision, but its communication and discussion are placed last on the meeting agenda. It is then allocated minimal discussion time and when supporters or implementors speak to the decision or action, the leader exhibits disinterest or a lack of enthusiasm for their contribution or for any serious commitment to a process of discernment. Following the presentation or discussion, no special affirmation is offered, and the leader reserves allocating resources and allows opposition without offering support. Such messaging of non-support is the surest way to kill off any action or decision, for the group forms the understanding that the proposal and decision have little hope of survival. Championing the decision requires the reverse: giving priority on meeting agenda placement and time allocation; introducing, supporting, affirming and celebrating contributions about the decision or action and demonstrating personal ownership of both the decision and the implementors. Expressed and demonstrated leadership is about communicating interest and support for the right decision, an essential element in the successful completion of decision action and change.

## An example from life

To conclude, another small real-life example of the strategy.

> After morning briefing with a secondary school's 120 staff, the principal is met by the school's union organiser demanding that the principal expel James, a Year 9 student, who has been physically aggressive to students at the railway station after school. The union organiser is followed by the school counsellor pleading a second (or is it a third?) chance for the student. In between these conversations, the principal's mobile phone is ringing (she notes it is her 15-year-old son), the secretary is hovering and according to her diary (she says), the principal should be on her way to head office for a meeting.

This is a small example that can be translated into other contexts. How does a leader negotiate a way through the mess of leadership? Of course, she is not going to make a decision there and then ... at least not on this occasion! A helpful starting point in her decision-making, we suggest, is for the leader to acknowledge that her decision requires moral discernment, and we offer the strategies offered previously and here as a possible path towards resolution and action. Faced with such conflicting complexities, the leader needs to work through a process of identifying certain elements. For example, having recognised there are tensions, can she name them? Does she have access to information and facts around the tension and its different elements? Can she identify the values that are in tension, which can lead towards a weighing of priorities in values? Can she recognise the needs of various players involved?

In this relatively simple example, the principal is forced to recognise the tension between the union rep and the pastoral counsellor (Strategy #1);[21] both are operating from a values base: one from the value of providing a safe working environment for teachers, the other from the value of providing a caring environment for the offending student (#2). The principal will also recognise the needs of a range of people including teachers, James' parents, and the safety of all students (#5). Like the counsellor, the principal is aware of facts around the student, that he comes from a troubled family, has experienced a lot of trauma and dislocation in his life, and at last, in this school – despite his unacceptable behaviour on this and previous occasions – he is beginning to settle, to make friends and even to make academic progress. She is also aware that his transfer to another school would raise issues of travel which might put in jeopardy his continuing education (#2). With the counsellor, James' home room teacher, his parents and James himself, she will also canvas options and alternate courses of action (# 4, #5, #7) And underlying all of this is her personal commitment to lead a school which demonstrates the redemptive love of Jesus Christ (#6).

Approaches to leadership that emphasise the relational, transrelational and collaborative – which are all consistent with a synodal approach – would prefer the working-through being done in 'the group'. This will, of course, vary with the circumstances of a particular issue; sometimes it will be appropriate to work through some issues across a whole department, or even a whole

agency, but more often this is appropriate in smaller units or teams (#4, #8). In the simple example above, the principal also needs to decide who will be included in making the final decision about young James (#8). Underlying all of this are the principles at stake: justice to James, the common good, the best interests of the other students, and the rights of the staff to a safe environment (#7). Sometimes discernment will lead to a 'James' being expelled, but if the principal makes this decision after she and her colleagues have considered the various elements in the moral discernment strategy, it will be a decision that, while a compromise, is one she can more easily live with (#9), even if she still has the task of 'championing' the decision with staff – including the Counsellor (#10).

## Conclusion

This chapter has presented a generic strategy to guide decision-making that is complementary to the use of the Values and Purposes Taxonomy and the Moral Decision-Making Model. This can be utilised to assist in any decision-maker process that will encourage reflection that should test the morality, virtues and consequences of decisions.

## Activity 9.1: James, a case study

Read through the James case study presented at the end of this Chapter. Take the position of one of the people in the example.

- Discuss the Strategy for Moral Decision-Making outlined in the text and reach a decision based on the facts available.
- Justify your decision to a colleague and have them critique your rationale for reaching this decision. Change roles and repeat the process.
- Did this experience give you any insights into the elements of the strategy?

## Activity 9.2: Moral decision-making in governance

In her study on the governance of human service organisations in the Catholic Church in Australia[22], Maureen Cleary identified a number of dilemmas that present for resolution by those in governance in Church:

- balancing the charism of a religious institute with Catholic identity
- discerning what makes church services ministry distinctive from other services offering the same service and care from a secular base
- shifting governance from an historically embedded non-synodal decision-making approach to one that is more synodal
- the integration by governing Boards into their decision-making of religious beliefs and business aspects.[23]

Use the Strategy for Moral Decision-Making to analyse one or more of the four dilemmas presented above, given your personal experience of such circumstances.

If you are in a group, first work individually and then discuss your analysis with the group. You may lack the necessary details to complete some requisites but attempt the full process so as to gain as much insight into the process as possible.

## Endnotes

1. A.Bandura, Selective moral disengagement in the exercise of moral agency, *Journal of Moral Education*, 31:2, 2002, p. 101.
2. Burford & Pettit, 2018.
3. See James R. Rest, *Development in Judging Moral Issues*, University of Minnesota Press, 1992.
4. B. Dotger & G. Theoharis, From disposition to action: bridging moral/ethical reasoning and social justice leadership, *Values and Ethics in Educational Administration*, 6:3, 2008, pp. 1-8.
5. Tuana, 2007, p. 375.
6. F. Tomazin, Schools caught cheating on NAPLAN, *Sydney Morning Herald*, 12 February 2013, p. 27, retrieved from http://www.smh.com.au
7. M. Bezzina, Moral purpose: A blind spot in ethical leadership?, paper presented at the 16th Annual Values and Leadership Conference, Victoria, BC, Sept. 25-27, 2011. p. 3.
8. M. Fullan, *The moral imperative realized*, Corwin Press, Thousand Oaks, California, 2010, p. 15.
9. Bezzina & Tuana, 2012, p. 6.
10. Major General Adam Findlay, General speaks out over atrocities, *Sydney Morning Herald*, 29 June 2020, p. 6.
11. Bezzina, & Tuana,
12. W. C. Frick, S. C. Faircloth & K. S. Little, Responding to the collective and individual best interests of students: Revisiting the tension between administrative practice and ethical imperatives in special education leadership, *Educational Administration Quarterly*, 49:2, 2013, pp. 207-242.
13. These issues were identified by Maureen Cleary in research associated with her publication *Management Dilemmas in Catholic Human Service: Health Care, Welfare, and Education*, The Edwin Mellen Press, 2007. ProQuest Ebook Central, http://ebookcentral.proquest.com/lib/acu/detail.action?docID=992490, accessed 7 May 2020.
14. The numbers are for convenience of reference rather than to suggest any lock-step progression.
15. C. M. Branson, M. Franken, and D. Penney, Reconceptualising Middle Leadership in Higher Education: A Transrelational Approach, in *Values and virtues in higher education research: Critical perspectives*, J. McNiff (ed), Rutledge, Abington, 2016, pp. 155-170.
16. Archbishop Mark Coleridge, 2019.
17. See D. Goleman.
18. A miracle, no less – and on prime-time TV – as Jesuit sees the light, *Sydney Morning Herald*, 4th July, 2003, https://www.smh.com.au/opinion/a-miracle-no-less-and-on-prime-time-tv-as-jesuit-sees-the-light-20030704-gdh1c1.html
19. The numbers in parentheses refer to the Strategies for the Moral Discernment Model in Ch. 5.
20. Margaret Wheatley, 2006, p. 131.
21. Numbers refer to the strategies for moral discernment presented in Chapter 5.
22. Maureen Cleary, *Management Dilemmas in Catholic Human Service: Health Care, Welfare, and Education*, The Edwin Mellen Press, 2007. ProQuest Ebook Central, http://ebookcentral.proquest.com/lib/acu/detail.action?docID=992490, accessed 7 May 2020.
23. See Maureen Cleary, Ch 6. The author diligently explores the development and character of governance in the Catholic Church in Australia from its colonial foundations. In something of an understatement, she later sums up the exercise of authority in the Catholic Church as having been *dominated historically by an authoritarian decision-making style by the bishops, clergy and leaders of religious institutes.*

# Chapter 10

# Developing Leadership for a Synodal Church

The purpose of this text has been to investigate the nature of leadership in a Church that lives out its synodality, and to identify some of the challenges for present and future leaders in such a Church.

Initially we attempted to uncover the foundational mission of our church and how it relates to the present context of the Church and its leadership. Next we analysed the Church as a culture of a people of faith, and how such a culture could reflect synodal relationships and leadership. To help us with this analysis we investigated contemporary views of leadership as a transrelational and moral process and how this defined what a synodal culture in the Church would look like. We then attempted to demonstrate how such a culture would be experienced in governance, leadership, people and processes; especially in discernment and resolution of moral issues and decision-making. The journey led us to reinforcing the central place of leadership in maintaining and renewing a synodal culture for our Church, and to uncovering the kind of beliefs, understandings and practices that would be essential in the development of such leaders.

In this chapter we will attempt to meet the crucial challenge of what to do about this recognition through the creation of a leadership development program for clergy and other leaders in the Church. The consistent theme emerging from Church literature, research and opinions over the past five years is that the need for a culture of leadership that fits a synodal Church is a critical need. It is no longer an option: it is an imperative.

While there are probably many ways to enhance leadership that is 'in and of' a synodal Church, we recommend an approach that is consistent with the challenges identified in the text. The development program should focus on leadership in the Church for ordained and commissioned leaders with a generic leadership core for all participants and context-specific elements related to each area of ministry. The development program should have formal and systematic approaches that are enriched by other less formal and more episodic initiatives. And it should include all those in leadership roles. The objective of the program should be the development of Church leaders who understand and practise synodality in building up a more synodal Church.

## Leadership development

The text showed how we live in an era when leadership can sometimes be seen as the panacea for the resolution of all organisation problems and challenges, and as such its practice has become increasingly nuanced. New understandings and practices have helped to shape the exercise of leadership not only in secular organisations, but in many of the Church's principal ministries in health, welfare and education. This has, however, been less evident in the exercise of clerical and pastoral leadership. Some senior clergy in the past may have been unsure of how to access research and literature on 'leadership' and so have neglected a valuable tool because they did not fully understand its scope and potential to serve their ministry. Some leaders in the Church have blamed their lack of business and organisational know-how for the current crisis, but we have suggested it is a lack of leadership capacity and understanding that has contributed to this situation. Some have turned to legal authority for assurance. Now is not the time to shore up the Church's legal defences; to rely on such tools is to ignore the elephant in the room. It is time to continue to refocus on our mission, empowered with the valuable tools of leadership based on a biblical model and orientation.

There are a number of agencies offering short and longer-term courses in one or other aspect of ministry preparation and leadership. We offer the following as scaffolding for leadership development for those in the Church. The focus of our suggestions is on developing leadership for a synodal Church and so deliberately we do not include other elements that could be useful (depending on roles) such as theology, ministry, governance, canon law or business management.

## Underlying principles

The leadership program here takes its framework from the research and analysis contained in the text. It is based on certain guiding principles which we believe should be observed and incorporated in this, and any program with a similar goal. The framework guidelines are:

- Programs in leadership development will be formal and systemic.

- Courses will be developed in such a way that the processes contribute to a developing 'shared wisdom' about leadership for mission across the Church.

- Leadership development courses will be directed towards all formal leadership roles, and appropriately engage those already in, or those entering into, these roles.

- The experiences, prior knowledge and reflections of all participants are valued content and resources for the program.

- The process of learning together is seen as an integral element of the proposed program. Processes will emphasise participants coming together from across all areas of ministry, including the ordained, women and men, experienced and less experienced, to complete programs in concert with each other. Engaging together in hearing, learning, reflecting on and applying the study of leadership can further break down false distinctions between 'clergy' and 'lay'.

- The program's processes will model a Church oriented to mutuality and partnership, synodality, co-responsibility, inclusion and subsidiarity, and so it will be developed in consultation and collaboration with the full range of potential participants and in conjunction with existing resources and structures.

- The program will employ a range of learning approaches that meet the different qualifications, experiences, learning styles and roles of participants.

- Prayer and reflection together will be an essential element of the process.

- Ongoing feedback and a formal evaluation of the program's approach and content would be built into the process.

## Focus of outcomes

The focus of this proposed course in leadership development will be for participants to build on their experience and knowledge, to reflect, to engage together and to develop further:

- understandings of contemporary research and theory on leadership, how these have changed, and the implications for those in ministries,

- language and understandings of cultural leadership that is synodal: meaning inclusive, open to the Spirit, collaborative, transrelational, in dialogue, mission and service-oriented, and involving processes of shared decision-making and moral discernment

| Focus Area | Content |
| --- | --- |
| Leadership for mission | - Mission of the Church<br>- Ministries at the service of mission<br>- Scriptural foundations for ministries<br>- Clarifying one's moral and religious purpose as a leader in ministry<br>- Awareness and growth of the interior self<br>- Developing a spirituality for leadership for mission, drawing on scriptural traditions, narratives, disciplines and virtue<br>- Sustaining oneself as a leader; practical tools for greater effectiveness |
| Cultural leadership for a synodal Church | - Culture of organisations, with special reference to the Church<br>- Understanding leadership and culture<br>- Synodality and the Church<br>- Leading for a synodal culture in the Church<br>- Leading change and renewal |
| Lessons from leadership theory | - Historical development of leadership theory<br>- Ethical and moral leadership<br>- Transrelational leadership in a Church setting |
| Building synodality through leadership | - Governance<br>- People-related processes in a synodal Church<br>- Building synodal communities |
| Moral discernment and decision-making | - Values and Purpose Taxonomy as a tool for discernment<br>- Moral and personal purposes influencing leadership<br>- Organisational challenges and dilemmas for leaders<br>- Challenges from external culture and context<br>- Challenges in the context of a future Church<br>- Strategy for moral decision-making |

Table 10.1 Focus and content for proposed leadership development course

- theological understandings of participants' areas of ministry as leadership, understanding this in a way that helps each leader sustain their own leadership and support the leadership of others,
- understandings of how to effect cultural shifts within different areas of ministry,
- understandings of planning for mission,
- ways to express their accountability to the Word, their communities, and the Church's mission,
- understandings of how to strengthen community'
- planning for the emergence of future leaders in each area of ministry, and the capacity to share understandings and reflections with other participants

| Model A<br>4 residential sessions | Model B<br>1 residential, 4-5 days' intensive sessions + concluding day | Model C<br>2 residentials<br>4 days each |
|---|---|---|
| Module 1: Arrive evening for opening session, prayer, meal, community-building, followed by 2 full days in residence. | Arrive evening for opening session, prayer, meal, community-building, followed by Day 1 session. | Module 1: Arrive evening for opening session, prayer, meal, community-building, followed by 4 full days in residence. |
| Module 2: Arrive evening for opening session, prayer, meal, community-building, followed by 2 full days in residence | Sessions Days 2-6: intensive 5 days (non-residential) supported by on-line follow-up. | |
| Module 3: Arrive evening for opening session, prayer, meal, community-building, followed by 2 full days in residence. | Concluding session Day 7: evening gathering followed by full day session. | Module 2 (after 1-2 months): Arrive evening for opening session, prayer, meal, community-building, followed by 4 full days in residence. |
| Module 4: Arrive evening for opening session, prayer, meal, community-building, followed by 1 full day in residence. | | |

Table 10.2 Possible models for a leadership development program

## Design and implementation

The learning processes would be varied. For example, they could include readings, discussion, formal presentations, learning teams, case studies, applied papers in both on-line and face-to-face sessions. Participants could also be expected to complete individual and group projects.

To illustrate the possibilities, possible formats for a full program could be organised according to the needs of participants in various arrangements. The table above illustrates three examples of a program conducted over a year. Notionally, the total time involved is estimated at around eight days.

To implement such a formal proposal, consideration could be given to engaging a suitable provider. Australian Catholic University is just one such provider, amongst others, such as BBI The Australian Institute of Theological Education (BBI-TAITE). The authors are not presuming that this text is the definitive or only reference point for the development of such programs.

The authors do not take ownership of the framework provided and simply propose it for consideration by anyone looking to develop such a program. There are many within different Church agencies who can contribute.

## Examples of similar leadership development programs

A program such as proposed here is not without precedents that have been planned, conducted and evaluated. We cite three examples briefly in which the authors have previously been involved in designing, teaching and coordinating.

### Anglicare Leadership Development Program

This was a bespoke program co-developed and conducted with Sydney Anglicare. The program involved more than 50 leaders and managers of the welfare administration of Anglicare between 2006-2009. One particular significance of this program was the sensitive interaction and co-leadership of the program between the Sydney Anglican church and Australian Catholic University in a way that respected the Anglican input on theology modules. Each iteration of the program ran over six 2-day modules incorporating readings, academic input, practical exercises, and prayer and formation. It was premised on a values-oriented conception of leadership. A group project involving leaders from across different areas of Anglicare was part of the process. Credit was available to those who completed the requirements as per ACU's Masters-level units.

A formal independent evaluation commented on the success of the program particularly with respect to building leadership capacity.

### ELIM Leadership Program

ELIM was a unique leadership development opportunity for Catholic school principals and education system leaders. It ran between 1994 and 2018. Initiated by the Diocese of Parramatta, the program worked cooperatively with other dioceses and ACU. The program combined engagement with the latest educational thinking, a deepening of the religious dimension of Catholic schools, the opportunity for quiet, reflection and active professional and personal encounter in prayerful community in a residential program conducted in total over two weeks, but throughout a period of some months. The best key speakers were engaged, both from within Australia and from overseas.

Structured feedback from cohorts was overwhelmingly positive, with special affirmation that the formula of two separate residentials provided a powerful learning and transformational experience for the hundreds of participants.

### Ministry Leadership Program (MLP)

The MLP is designed for Catholic health, aged care and social services leaders to ensure the healing ministry of the Church remains faithful to the spirit of the Gospel. The program targets the most senior leaders to enable those with decision making responsibility to drive a mission-driven culture. The Ministry Leadership Program is a highly practical formation program where in-session learnings are immediately applied on return to the workplace. The pedagogy centres on dialogue between the wisdom of the Catholic Tradition, the insights from contemporary culture, and the realities of personal/communal experience. Each session offers insight into a particular set of values and concerns of the Catholic tradition and invites participants to make connections to their leadership knowledge and experience, and the day-to-day responsibilities and challenges they face. The mutual understanding and trust developed through the diverse cross-sector engagement builds a sector wide 'community of leaders'. Together, these leaders are better able to collaborate in support of the mission.

Commenced under Catholic Health Australia in 2017, MLP has been conducted under the auspices of Australian Catholic University (ACU) since mid-2020. Now into its third cohort of 40 leaders, evaluation data indicates a high degree of satisfaction. Participants affirm their exposure to the richness of the Catholic intellectual and spiritual tradition in a content-rich but practically relevant way; the opportunities for personal and group reflection on content, as well as its application and integration with their leadership practice; and the access to the 'language of mission' that enables them to meaningfully address workplace challenges through the lens of the Catholic vision. The program currently runs over a 15-month period and recruitment is underway for the fourth cohort commencing in early 2021.

### Australian Leadership Awards

Four Projects (2007-2014) were funded through the Australian Government AusAID to develop leaders and aspiring leaders from various international organisations from Cambodia, Vietnam, East Timor, PNG, Laos, India, Philippines, Nepal, Tonga and Kiribati. Each project incorporated the identification of needs within sectors in the home country, sourcing and interviewing of applicants with participant organisations, development of proposals with full costings to AusAID, implementation and administration of projects in Australia and delivery in 28 days. In addition to courses shaped to participants' requirements, the program included the professional placement of participants with leader mentors in organisations similar to their home placement.

Each project was independently evaluated, and full reports presented to AusAID.

### Millennial Principals Project and Lutheran Principals Program

This program was conducted in collaboration with Lutheran Schools Australia from 2002-2015. The project included co-researching the needs of aspiring leaders in Lutheran schools across Australia. This was done using an interactive electronic methodology for the purpose of developing a Leadership Framework for Lutheran School Principals and aspiring leaders. The framework was the centrepiece of a leadership development program co-developed with Lutheran Schools of Australia. It incorporated: identification and selection of aspiring leaders: identification and training of principal mentors; designing learning activities incorporating national conferences, workshops, action research, and individual development profiling; and access to learning modules from tertiary institutions. The profiling of participants included action research projects and professional development plans for a three-year period.

The program was evaluated using an external evaluation company. The success of the initial program led to three iterations being conducted over 10 years.

### Supplementary Policies and Procedures

Certain policies and procedures about leadership practice should also be considered as part of leadership development in diocesan, parish, congregational or agency approaches to a synodal Church. We see the theory and practice of these policies as part of the curriculum outlined above, but their supplementary establishment would help support the goal of the program of leadership development.

### Mentoring in leadership in a synodal church

All those new to a role should be mentored in that role by someone of experience. This applies to people of experience

taking up new roles, such as priests coming from overseas, as much as it does to a newly appointed Pastoral Associate being linked with someone more experienced in a similar parish.

### *Ongoing supervision for growth in leadership*
We believe that all those in formal leadership roles should be supported through induction, ongoing formation and coaching, supervision and debriefing. The experience of being left to 'sink or swim' in a leadership role in the Church can be destructive and counter-productive. It minimises the potential outcomes from the person's work and can often lead to unhappy endings and wasted talent.

### Ongoing professional learning
Provision should be in place for regular and continuous learning by anyone engaged in an area of ministry, as is the practice and expectation in most workplaces and in every profession. Policies relating to expectations about ongoing learning can support this. One such policy, for example, would be the annual investment of a certain amount of time in ongoing learning. This needs to be supported by budget provisions that are available to all in leadership roles in the Church.

### Regular time for renewal
The time-honoured practice of religious institutes and clergy allocating a specified time each year to spiritual reflection and or direction is a valuable legacy that should be shared with all those in leadership roles. In some dioceses, this practice has been implemented by some Catholic Education offices, and the creation of 'spirituality teams' or the provision of 'spirituality days' have been allocated to school principals each year.

Likewise, in Ministerial PJPs the commitment to renewal has been programmed regularly for leaders across the ministries.

### Regular performance appraisal.
Leadership development is supported by sound systems of performance feedback and review. Processes of review (or appraisal) should be available for all leaders in the Church. Not only is this an opportunity for the individual to receive clear feedback on their performance, including affirmation for achievements, sound appraisal processes allow for the leader to plan ongoing emphases and future priorities in their role. It also allows for the leader to be supported by appropriate learning programs. Appraisal also offers an expression of accountability and transparency to the communities in which the leader serves and to the larger mission of the Church.

### Clinical supervision
For those involved in pastoral counselling roles, some kind of clinical supervision could be considered.

### Resource implications
Clearly, a proposal of this nature has significant resource implications and may be better undertaken through networking by dioceses or as an initiative of State and/or Federal Church bodies (such as the Australian Bishops Council, the National Catholic Education Commission, CatholicCare, Catholic Religious Australia and others). There are costs involved in the initiation of such programs for leaders, but we suggest the message from our text is that there are considerable costs in doing nothing. A proposal such as this should be seen as an investment in the future of our Church.

## In conclusion

There is a rich body of research and thinking about leadership that can be put at the service of the Church's mission. No one approach is a panacea; growth, development and cultural change are slow and require a range of strategies of which this text might be just one small part. Deep and sustained change usually comes slowly.

The conversation we have had here about faith-based, mission-oriented synodal leadership of a church in the spirit of Vatican II needs to engage all those in formal leadership roles. This needs to be done together around the same table, enriching each other for a shared journey.

This moment in the Church's life is a moment of hope, a point of transition. To invoke his words again in conclusion, Archbishop Coleridge said in his homily in Rome in February 2019, '... the time for words is past; now is the time for action'.[1] We believe we can and must act now. We trust this text may contribute in some small way to this journey forward.

## Endnote

[1] Archbishop Mark Coleridge, President ACBC, homily final Mass, meeting on The Protection of Minors in the Church, Rome, 21-24 February, 2019.

# Acknowledgements

We are indebted to many people who have contributed to this book. Given the extensive and complex structures that exist in the services and ministries of the Australian Catholic Church, we sought the advice and guidance of experts and leaders in the fields of theology, education, social services, health, welfare and governance in regard to the accuracy and worthiness of our manuscript. We are deeply appreciative of their generosity in reading the text and for sharing their insights and wisdom with us. We found their support affirming and inspiring. While their contributions have given us the confidence to offer the book for your consideration, any errors of fact or interpretation are entirely our own work. Specifically, we thank the following for their professional and personal commitment to our work:

Dr Lauretta Baker RSJ

Philomena Billington

Teresa Brierley

Dr Maureen Cleary

Sr Patty Fawkner SGS

Professor David Hall FMS

Dr Tessa Ho

David Hutton

Rev Joseph Lam

Rev Richard Lennan

Paul McClintock

Kath McCormack

Padmi Pathinather

Dr Lee-Anne Perry AM

Philip Pogson

Rev David Ranson

Dr Kevin Treston OAM

We also wish to acknowledge and thank our colleagues and friends who joined the original conversation in response to the writings and challenges of Bishop Vincent Long of the Diocese of Parramatta that inspired the development of this book: Dr Michael Bezzina, Patricia Crennan, Aengus Kavanagh fsp, Brenda Kennedy chf, Elizabeth O'Callaghan, Vic O'Callaghan, Leone Palliser OSU, and Greg Wilson.

Thank you to our friends at Garratt Publishing for their professional and friendly support, especially Garry Eastman for his vision and commitment in extending the invitation to us to publish on this topic. Garry expressed a robust dedication to the Church through decades of creativity and professionalism in publishing and we join others in mourning his recent death. Thanks also to Karen Tayleur, Gregory Hill and their colleagues for their patience and guidance throughout the publishing process.

Finally, we offer thanks to our partners Susai Benjamin and Dianne Burford for their support and understanding of our commitment to this task.

# List of Activities

1.1: Who is Jesus?, p12

1.2: What is tenderness?, p13

2.1: For reflection and discussion, p22

3.1: What are my values?, p29

3.2: Possible assumptions regarding leadership arising from misalignments of mission values and culture in the Church, p29

3.3: Building your leadership credo, p29

4.2: Building collaborative communities, p37

5.1: Effective leaders, p47

5.2: Transrelational leaders, p47

5.3: Working at our best, p47

6.1: Messages about culture, p55

7.1: Activity p63

8.1: Ethics in leadership, p70

8.2: Interior reflection, p71

8.3: Power in leadership, p71

9.1: James, a case study, p81

9.2: Moral decision-making in governance, p81

# List of Diagrams, Figures & Tables

Figure 3.1: Values Aligned Model, p27

Figure 5.1: Domains of leadership, p40

Figure 5.2: Hersey-Blanchard: Situational leadership theory (SLT), p41

Figure 5.3: Starratt's vision for cultural leadership, p42

Figure 5.4: Contrasting leadership models, p47

Diagram 8.1: Values and taxonomy from Burford and Pettit, p66

Diagram 9.1: Moral decision-making, p74

Table 9.1: Requisites of moral decision-making, p75

Table 10.1 Focus and content for proposed leadership development course, p84

Table 10.2 Possible models for a leadership development program, p85

# Further Reading

Begley, P.T., Self-knowledge, Capacity and Sensitivity: Prerequisites to Authentic Leadership by School Principals, *Journal of Educational Administration,* 44:6, 2006, pp. 570-589.

Burns, J. M., *Leadership*, HarperCollins, New York, 2010.

Catholics for Renewal, *Getting Back on Mission*, Garratt Publishing, Melbourne, 2019.

Crothers, John, *The Clergy Club*, Garratt Publishing, Melbourne, 2018.

D'Orsa, Jim, & Therese D'Orsa with A. Brown, J. Meneely and Catholic Educators from the Ballarat Diocese, *Educator's Guide to Mission in Practice. Discipleship in Action in Catholic Schools*, Vaughan Publishing, Melbourne, 2019.

Duignan, P., *Educational Leadership: Key Challenges and Ethical Tensions*, Cambridge University Press, New York, 2006.

Faggioli, Massimo. Pope Francis' struggle to bring forth a synodal Church, *La Croix International*, 26 December 2018.

GRPT, The Light from the Southern Cross, Promoting co-responsible governance in the Catholic Church in Australia, Final Report of the Governance Review Project Team, August 2020.

Branson, C.M. & S.J. Gross (eds), *Handbook of Ethical Educational Leadership*, Routledge, New York, 2014.

International Theological Commission, *Sensus Fidei* in the life of the Church, 2014, http://www.vatican.va/roman_curia/congregations/cfaith/cti_documents/rc_cti_20140610_sensus-fidei_en.html

International Theological Commission, Synodality in the Life and Mission of the Church, International Theological Commission, 2018, http://www.vatican.va/roman_curia/congregations/cfaith/cti_documents/rc_cti_20180302_sinodalita_en.html#

Kavanagh, Aengus, fsp, (ed), *A Call to Re-set the Sails*, Plenary Council 2020, Patrician Brothers, 2020.

Lennan, Richard, Richard Gaillardetz et al, To serve the people of God: renewing the conversation on priesthood and ministry, Boston College Seminar on Priesthood and the Contemporary Church, Origins, 48:31, 2018.

Pope Francis, 2018, *Gaudete et Exultate, The call to holiness in today's world*, 19th March 2018.

Rush, Ormond, Plenary Council Participation and Reception: Synodality and Discerning the *Sensus Fidelium, Theological Studies* 78:2, 2017, pp. 295-325.

Rush, Ormond, *The Vision of Vatican II: its fundamental principles*, Liturgical Press, Collegeville, 2019.

Starratt, R., *Ethical Leadership*, John Wiley & Sons, San Francisco, 2004.

Pascoe, Susan, Best Practice in Governance of Church Agencies: Keynote Address delivered to the *Principles and Practice for Church Governance Conference*, Yarra Theological Union and University of Divinity, Melbourne, 2019, accessed 9 June, 2020, https://www.ampjps.org.au/wp-content/uploads/2019/03/Pascoe-Best-Practice-in-Governance-YTU-3Mar2019.pdf.

Tuana, N. Conceptualizing moral literacy, *Journal of Educational Administration*, 45:4, 2007, pp. 364-378.

Wheatley, M. J., *Leadership and the New Science: Discovering Order in a Chaotic World* (3rd ed.), Berrett-Koehler Publishers, San Francisco, 2006.

# About the Authors

Anne Benjamin DSG, BA(Hons), PhD (Religious Education), MA(Leadership), GAICD, FACE, FACEL, is an Honorary Fellow of UWS and Honorary Professor at ACU. Anne has 50 years' experience in teaching, administration, leadership, governance and consultancy in Education, Higher Education and Church across Australia, Tonga, Papua New Guinea, New Zealand and India. She has worked with PJPs, the Australian Council of Churches, the Lutheran Church of Australia and Sydney Anglicare. She served as Director of Schools in the Diocese of Parramatta from 1997-2005.

Anne's previous publications include: *Children of the Kingdom*, *Storymakers*, *Catholic Schools: Hope in Uncertain Times*, edited with Dan Riley. An anthology of biographies and essays, *Not Forgotten, Australian Catholic Educators 1820-2020*, co-edited with Seamus O'Grady, was published in December 2020 as the first publication in the *Biographical Dictionary of Australian Catholic Educators* project.

Charles Burford, Dip PE, B.Ed., M.Ed. (Admin), PhD (Educational Administration), FACEL, is an Honorary Professor at ACU. He has been an experienced teacher, administrator, academic and consultant in the University, Education, Health and Business sectors in Canada, U.S.A., Hong Kong, PNG, Tonga, Italy, Sweden and Australia for more than forty years. He developed and implemented ACU's first program for Catholic Educational Leaders in 1980. This grew into the largest post-graduate program in Educational Leadership in Australia and the Asia Pacific region. In 2008 he was awarded by the American University Council for Educational Administration (UCEA) the 2008 Willower Award of Excellence for his work in Ethics and Leadership.

www.ingramcontent.com/pod-product-compliance
Lightning Source LLC
Chambersburg PA
CBHW040317240426
43665CB00030B/2971